Endorsement

"Every parent who wants to raise godly children needs to use this book as guidance to cry out for their children. Because we are bringing up our children in a very toxic world with vicious ramifications and destructive bends, the uniqueness of this book will help parents and grandparents to pray for different aspects of children's lives. Every page is filled with insights based on the Scriptures. This book has already benefited hundreds, if not thousands, of parents."

—Steven Vuppula,
Director of Indian Outreach, Gate City Church,
Nashua, New Hampshire

Prayers to Restore Our Children By the Word of God

LEONIE SHANKAR

LUCIDBOOKS

Prayers to Restore Our Children By the Word of God

Published by Lucid Books in Houston, TX
www.LucidBooks.com

ISBN: 978-1-63296-738-1
eISBN: 978-1-63296-739-8

Special Sales: Most Lucid Books titles are available in special quantity discounts. Custom imprinting or excerpting can also be done to fit special needs. Contact Lucid Books at Info@LucidBooks.com

Dedication

To my Lord and Savior Jesus Christ, who is faithful to keep His promise.

To our New Hampshire Indian Christian Outreach Bible Study families, whose friendship has brought profound purpose and joy into my life.

By God's grace, may this book reach countless parents who feel compelled to pray for their children.

> *I am the Lord, the God of all flesh. Is there anything too hard for Me?*
>
> —Jeremiah 32:27

Special Thanks

Nothing is impossible with God.
—Luke 1:37 ESV

I thank and praise God for His unending grace.

I am deeply grateful to Steven Vuppula, the Leader of the New Hampshire Indian Christian Outreach Group, who encouraged me to write 31 days of prayer for children. His support was instrumental in sharing these prayers with our group's parents and publishing them in this prayer book. Sincere thanks to my husband, Sam Shankar, for his dedication and efforts in reaching this generation, and thanks also to our son, Joash Shankar, for his support.

The love and encouragement from our Indian outreach friends and families have been a source of strength. Finally, I cannot adequately express my gratitude to Pastor David Stewart Jr. for his impactful and practical messages that have significantly influenced my life.

Contents

Part III: For Their Life at School and Work

Part IV: For Their Commitment to God

Part V: For Their Spiritual Growth

Part VI: For Their Deliverance

Part VII: For Their Impact

Part VIII: Marriage

Part IX: Blessings

Appendix

Foreword

Our Lord Jesus declared, *"The thief cometh not, but for to steal, and to kill, and to destroy"* (John 10:10 KJV). Further, the Scriptures inform us that the last days will be marked by much deception and by a great falling away from faith (Matthew 24:4–14 and 2 Thessalonians 2:1–3).

The deception, so prevalent in the last days, will be especially targeted toward children and young people. You and your family must be prepared to stand against the demonic deception and weaponry arrayed against you.

There are two important spiritual disciplines that will sustain you and your family in these last days. First, you must read and know your Bible. Read the Bible daily, meditate in it, memorize it, but above all, live it. Live what it teaches.

The second important discipline is prayer. Prayer is the vital, life-giving communication available between God and man. Through prayer, we have the privilege of speaking to God, and the great joy of hearing, by His Spirit, from Him.

The book by Mrs. Leonie Shankar, which you are holding

in your hand, is focused on prayer. It will help you to pray strong and effectual prayers for your children and your family.

Leonie has not written this book from a theoretical perspective. She is a prayerful woman. She and her husband are faithful prayer warriors. The things that she has written in this book have been learned in her personal prayer closet praying for her own family.

The deception of the last days has already begun. It is critical that you give yourself to prayer for your children, your family, yourself, and for others whom you love. May God help all of us to pray with greater fervor and zeal for the glory and the honor of God's name.

In Christ Jesus,
David E. Stewart Jr.
Pastor of NewLife Church,
Leominster, Massachusetts

Preface

I thank and praise my Lord and Savior Jesus Christ who has enabled me to write this prayer book for God's glory. I never intended to write a book, but I thank God for the burden He placed on the heart of our New Hampshire Indian Outreach Bible Study group leader, Steven Vuppula, for this generation. Steven earnestly desires to encourage parents to pray for their children. He initially asked me to write 21 days of prayer for our Bible study group parents to use in praying for their children. I shared those prayers in our WhatsApp and Signal groups every day, and they, in turn, shared them with many other WhatsApp groups.

By God's grace, we received testimonies that many were blessed by those prayers. So, Steven suggested that I make it 31days of prayer for children. God birthed a vision in his heart to reach out to other parents, and this vision eventually led to publishing *Prayers to Restore Our Children by the Word of God*. I praise God that my husband Sam Shankar shares the same vision, and I am also thankful to God for our son Joash

Shankar for his support. I am greatly encouraged by the responses from my Bible study group friends and families.

There is a war going on for the souls of our children; the influence of secularism and cultural relativism has made parenting very difficult. Every parent struggles with fears and frustrations in raising their children, and many children have terrible relationships with their parents. When children go extreme and out of control, parents often experience feelings of depression, hopelessness, and incompetence. Sometimes, Christian parents feel unprepared and ill-equipped to raise their children in a godly way. Even though some Christian parents have waited for God by fasting and praying for their children, they might think that their prayers don't even get past the ceiling. But the purpose of this book is to encourage parents that we serve a sovereign God who is in control of our children.

> *He who made the ear, does He not hear? He who formed the eye, does he not see?*
>
> —Psalm 94:9 AMP

> *You keep track of all my sorrows. You have collected all my tears in your bottle. You have recorded each one in your book.*
>
> —Psalm 56:8 NLT

Raising godly children does not just happen; it is the result of fervent prayer and hard work on the part of both parents. We must acknowledge that this generation faces more distractions than previous generations—distractions that can potentially rob them of their God-given identity. Often, when parents are fighting against their children in the natural realm, they fail to understand that there is a spiritual aspect to their struggle (Ephesians 6:10–18). My desire here is to provide some guidance for the parents to pray for their children according to God's promises in His Word. I certainly believe that God's word will restore hope to parents who have lost hope: *"And in His word I do hope"* (Psalm 130:5b).

Prayer and promises are interdependent. Without the promise prayer is eccentric and baseless. Without prayer, the promise is dim, voiceless, shadows, and impersonal. The promise inspires and energizes prayer, but prayer locates the promise, and gives it realization and location.[1]

Introduction

God is all-powerful and all-knowing. He knows the conditions of our hearts. He is aware of all our ways and shortcomings. Yet, He loves us unconditionally. We all experience tests and challenges in life. In times of uncertainty, we feel like nobody can understand us. But Jesus sympathizes with us, for He faced all the same testing we do, yet without sin (Hebrews 4:15). He knows how it feels when we are hurt, humiliated, or in pain. *"Since he himself has gone through suffering and testing, he is able to help us when we are being tested"* (Hebrews 2:18 NLT). Jesus's death on the cross for our sins made a way for us to have a relationship with God; otherwise, we would be separated from God.

God's Word says, *"Let us therefore come boldly to the throne of grace, that we may obtain mercy and find grace to help in time of need"* (Hebrews 4:16). Jim Cymbala explains that "it is not a throne of judgment for us to fear. Because of His mercy, we do not get the punishment that we deserve, and because of His grace, we get the good things that we don't deserve."[2] God will listen to the earnest cry of a person who is in need. We have the assurance that we can come to Him without hesitancy or trembling but with confidence. He is a compassionate God who bestows His goodness and grace upon us. If we believe and ask according to God's will, we can have the confidence that our prayers will be answered (1 John 5:14). What is not possible by human efforts is possible with God.

There is a fierce battle over this generation, and the enemy is warring against them on every side. He hinders their walk with God and influences them to believe that their self-worth and identity are based on their outside appearance. They are constantly bombarded with negative messages. Families are devastated and torn apart as they raise their children. God's Word says, *"Train up a child in the way he should go, and when he is old, he will not depart from it"* (Proverbs 22:6). No child is perfect. Parents need to ask the Lord to intervene in their children's lives so that they will not be entangled in the things of this world. There is a profound truth in the Scripture that says, *"You do not have because you do not ask"* (James 4:2b). We have the privilege of approaching God to submit our requests for our children. I encourage you to remain in expectancy and faith for their salvation and their walk with God. When we do not know how to pray, the Holy Spirit will help us to pray according to the will of God (Romans 8:26–27).

God spoke, and the world came into existence (Hebrews 11:3). When we align our prayer with the Word of God, it will have a lasting impact on our children's lives. As we confidently declare God's Word, we confess that we agree with what God says and that it shall be carried out according to God's will and purpose. *"You will also decree a thing, and it will be established for you"* (Job 22:28a NASB 1995). May the Lord make us more fervent in prayer and anchored in His Word.

Charles Stanley famously said, "Fight all your battles on your knees, and you win every time."[3]

God has great plans for your children. Whatever battle you are facing, never lose hope. God is well able to restore (bring them back, renew, and make whole) our children to His original intent.

Part I

For the Condition of Their Hearts

DAY 1

Prayer for a Heart to Seek God

And you will seek Me and find Me, when you search for Me with all your heart.

—Jeremiah 29:13

Many seek after a god, but not always after the true God. According to God's Word, eternal life is to know the true God and His Son Jesus Christ (John 17:3). As we seek God, we can hear His voice. As we seek God, we can understand His plan for His Children. God's word says that as long as King Uzziah sought the Lord, God gave him success (2 Chronicles 26:5b).

Charles Stanley explains how we are to seek God. He says:

> It begins with studying His Word and trusting in Him. If our focus is set on the things of earth, our

> desires will bend in that direction. But if we turn our attention to the Word of God, our desires for Him will become stronger than all other longings.[4]

John Piper adds, "Love for the world pushes out love for the Father."[5]

Prayer:

Lord, I surrender (CHILD'S NAME) into Your loving hands. I praise You, for You are the God who rewards those who earnestly seek You (Hebrews 11:6b). Please forgive the moments that (CHILD'S NAME) did not seek Your presence. Forgive (CHILD'S NAME) for the moments he/she chased after the pleasures of this world that lead to empty pursuit. Thank You for Your promise, that "*You have not forsaken those who seek You*" (Psalm 9:10b). Enable (CHILD'S NAME) to draw near to You with his/her whole heart (Psalm 119:2b). Direct his/her heart toward Your love (2 Thessalonians 3:5). As (CHILD'S NAME) begins to seek You, help him/her to hear Your voice clearly. Father, instill a desire in (CHILD'S NAME)'s heart to long for Your presence. Put Your fear in (CHILD'S NAME)'s heart so that he/she will not depart from You (Jeremiah 32:40 b). In Jesus's name, Amen!

Decree:

I declare and decree that (CHILD'S NAME) will not seek the things of this world that lead to disaster and emptiness, but rather seek the Lord and His ways with all his/her heart (Jeremiah 29:13).

Additional Scripture References to Seek God:

- *"The Lord is with you while you are with Him. If you seek Him, He will be found by you; but if you forsake Him, He will forsake you"* (2 Chronicles 15:2b).
- *"Thus says the Lord, the Holy One of Israel, and his Maker: "Ask Me of things to come concerning My sons; and concerning the work of My hands, you command Me"* (Isaiah 45:11).
- *"Draw near to God and He will draw near to you"* (James 4:8a NASB).
- *"Call to Me, and I will answer you, and show you great and mighty things, which you do not know"* (Jeremiah 33:3).

DAY 2

Prayer for Humility

Before his downfall a man's heart is proud, but humility comes before honor.

—Proverbs 18:12 HCSB

Consider these reflections on the role that pride and humility play in our lives:

> Pride is a vision problem that we all struggle with. In our pride, we fail to see our true place in God's scheme of things. Thinking that we are superior, we nurture contempt for others. Humility is the antidote to pride. True humility means seeing our place in relation to God and the world He has made.[6]

Humility is the one virtue we know we need but if we ever suggest we have it we only prove we don't. Jesus never resisted the sinner who repented, but he resisted those who were proud. Pride affects every area of our lives. Pride kills. We should pray about our tendency toward pride and seek to humble ourselves before God. Humility simply means to recognize our need for God. The way up is the way down.[7]

Prayer:

Lord, I surrender (CHILD'S NAME) into Your hands. Your word says that pride hardens the heart (Daniel 5:20) and that You desire compassion in (CHILD'S NAME) (Ephesians 4:32). Forgive (CHILD'S NAME) for the moments he/she thought too highly of himself/herself. Your Word says that Jesus emptied Himself and took the form of a bond servant (Philippians 2:7). Give (CHILD'S NAME) a humble spirit to serve You and value others above himself/herself (Philippians 2:3b). I renounce every manifestation of pride in every area of (CHILD'S NAME)'s life. Help (CHILD'S NAME) to understand that every good thing he/she enjoys in this life comes from You. Teach (CHILD'S NAME) to be humble and pour out Your grace upon him/her (James 4:6). In Jesus's name, Amen!!

Decree:

I declare and decree that pride and arrogance don't have a place in (CHILD'S NAME)'s heart. He/She will have a heart that seeks to exalt God (Psalm 46:10).

Additional Scripture References for Humility:

- *"If anyone desires to be first, he shall be last of all and servant of all"* (Mark 9:35b).
- *"By humility and the fear of the Lord are riches and honor and life"* (Proverbs 22:4).

- *"Pride goes before destruction, and a haughty spirit before a fall"* (Proverbs 16:18).
- *"Humble yourselves in the sight of the Lord, and He will lift you up"* (James 4:10).

DAY 3

Prayer to Forgive Others

Forgive us our sins, for we also forgive everyone who sins against us.

—Luke 11:4a NIV

There are many definitions of forgiveness, but a simple one is to surrender the right to hurt others in response to the way they've hurt us. It is refusing to retaliate or hold bitterness against people for the ways they have wounded us. We cannot hold on to bitterness and hold on to God.[8]

Forgiveness is the most powerful thing in the world. It can change not just our heart but also our entire way of life. It can go down to the deep and hidden roots of old and long-buried hurts.[9]

Bitterness is like a rock thrown into a placid pond; after its initial splash it sends out circular ripples that affect the whole pond. It starts with ourselves, expands to our spouse, then to our children, friends, and anyone we come in contact with.[10]

We must understand that God wants us to forgive others for our well-being. When we forgive, we experience freedom.

Prayer:

Father, I praise You, for You are faithful to forgive and cleanse us of our sins. I surrender (CHILD'S NAME) and all his/her hurts and pain into Your loving hands. Lord, according to Your Word, love is not easily angered, and love keeps no record of wrongs (1 Corinthians 13:5b). Please fill (CHILD'S NAME)'s heart with Your love through the power of the Holy Spirit that enables (CHILD'S NAME) to forgive others (Romans 5:5). Help (CHILD'S NAME) not to harbor bitterness and unforgiveness in his/her heart. Lord, show me the areas where (CHILD'S NAME) walks in the darkness of resentment. I bind every spirit of hatred and bitterness in (CHILD'S NAME)'s life in the name of Jesus, and I release (CHILD'S NAME) into Your hands. Uproot everything in (CHILD'S NAME)'s heart that is not of You. Impart in (CHILD'S NAME) the truth that if (he/she) forgives others, You are gracious enough to forgive (his/her) sins (Matthew 6:14). In Jesus's name, Amen!

Decree:

I declare and decree that (CHILD'S NAME) will walk in the freedom of God's forgiveness in his/her life. (CHILD'S NAME) will become a person who is quick to forgive and love others (Ephesians 4:32).

Additional Scripture References for Forgiveness:

- *"Bear with one another and forgive any complaint you may have against someone else. Forgive as the Lord forgave you"* (Colossians 3:13 BSB).
- *"Hatred stirs up strife, But love covers all sins"* (Proverbs 10:12).
- *"He is so rich in kindness and grace that he purchased our freedom with the blood of his Son and forgave our sins"* (Ephesians 1:7 NLT).
- *"Look after each other so that none of you fails to receive the grace of God. Watch out that no poisonous root of bitterness grows up to trouble you, corrupting many"* (Hebrews 12:15 NLT).

DAY 4

Prayer for Obedience

If anyone loves Me, he will keep My word.

—John 14:23a

Many blessings are tied to our obedience to God. *"Blessed are all who fear the Lord, who walk in obedience to him"* (Psalm 128:1 NIV). We can measure our love for Christ by our total obedience to Him. The Word of God says, *"You are My friends if you do what I command"* (NIV, John 15:14). John Piper says that "the Lord delights far more in obedience than in the performance of worship ceremonies without it."[11] Chambers observes:

> Our Lord never insists on obedience. He stresses very definitely what we ought to do, but He never forces us to do it. We have to obey Him out of a oneness of spirit with Him. The Lord does not give me rules, but He makes His standards very clear. If my relationship with Him is that of love, I will do what He says without hesitation.[12]

Prayer:

Father, I surrender (CHILD'S NAME) into Your hands and ask that You would enable (CHILD'S NAME) to obey

Your commandments. As Your Word says, give (CHILD'S NAME) a heart to obey his/her parents (Exodus 20:12). Lord, I thank You that Jesus was obedient to the point of death (Philippians 2:8). By the authority You've given me through the name of Jesus—the name above every name—I resist the spirit of rebellion and disobedience in (CHILD'S NAME)'s life. I bind every spirit that seeks to be in control and have its own way. I pray that (CHILD'S NAME)'s heart would be directed to obey Your commands. Lord, help (CHILD'S NAME) to walk in obedience to Your truth (3 John 1:4). Give (CHILD'S NAME) ears that are open to Your voice and a heart that is receptive to Your Word of truth (John 10:27). I submit (CHILD'S NAME) under Your authority and pray that he/she will be willing and obedient and enjoy Your blessings (Isaiah 1:19). In Jesus's name, Amen!

Decree:

I declare and decree that (CHILD'S NAME) will walk in obedience to God's Word. As (CHILD'S NAME) obeys and follows God's command, the Lord will set him/her high above all the nations on earth according to His Promise (Deuteronomy 28:1).

Additional Scripture References for Obedience:

- *"If you love me, obey my commandments"* (John 14:15 NLT).

- *"Obey me, and I will be your God and you will be my people. Walk in obedience to all I command you, that it may go well with you"* (Jeremiah 7:23b NIV).
- *"Children, obey your parents in the Lord, for this is right"* (Ephesians 6:1 NIV).
- *"If you fully obey the Lord your God and carefully follow all his commands I give you today, the Lord your God will set you high above all the nations on earth"* (Deuteronomy 28:1 NIV).

DAY 5

Prayer for Gratitude

And give thanks for everything to God the Father in the name of our Lord Jesus Christ.

—Ephesians 5:20 NLT

I have learned by experience that if I pause at every stage in life to acknowledge God, I can be confident that He will continue to direct my path (Proverbs 3:6). You might ask, "How can I acknowledge God?" The simplest and best way is to thank Him—and say "Thank You" for all He has done and for His faithfulness. You will get immediate assurance that He is going to continue to be faithful. Just as He has helped and guided you in the past, He will guide you in the future. But the key to this assurance is acknowledging Him by our thanksgiving.[13]

Prayer:

Father, I praise You and bless Your Holy Name for all Your goodness in (CHILD'S NAME)'s life. Lord, Your Word instructs us to be thankful in everything (1 Thessalonians 5:18). Thank You for all the blessings that You have showered in (CHILD'S NAME)'s life. Please remind (CHILD'S NAME) that every good and perfect gift comes from You (James 1:17). Give (CHILD'S NAME) a heart of gratitude and humility that gives honor to Your Name. Lord, please forgive the moments (CHILD'S NAME) failed to acknowledge Your goodness in his/her life. Father, as Your Word instructs, help (CHILD'S NAME) to do all things without murmuring and disputing (Philippians 2:14). I surrender the areas where (CHILD'S NAME) very often complains about little things. Please forgive (CHILD'S NAME) and give him/her a heart that overflows with gratitude. In Jesus's name, Amen!

Decree:

I declare and decree that (CHILD'S NAME) will offer thanksgiving and glorify God (Psalm 50:23a).

Additional Scripture References for Gratitude:

- *"And whatever you do in word or deed, do all in the name of the Lord Jesus, giving thanks to God the Father through Him"* (Colossians 3:17).
- *"Thanks be to God for His indescribable gift!"* (2 Corinthians 9:15).
- *"I will praise you, Lord, with all my heart; I will tell of all the marvelous things you have done"* (Psalm 9:1 NLT).
- *"Oh give thanks to the Lord, for he is good; for his steadfast love endures forever"* (Psalm 118:1 ESV)!

Part II

For Their Battles

DAY 6

Prayer for a Sound Mind

For God has not given us a spirit of fear, but of power and of love and of a sound mind.

— Timothy 1:7)

God has a wonderful life planned for every one of us, and He is concerned about the hidden man of the heart, which is our inner life. Our inner life is what we think about; the way we think determines how we live and who we are. Our mind is the battlefield. *"For as he thinks in his heart, so is he"* (Proverbs 23:7a). "You cannot have a positive life and a negative mind."[14]

Jentzen Franklin has these words of wisdom:

> Many people live their lives believing that they are intellectually inferior—born that way and will always be that way. The problem with believing this is that you begin to live accordingly. Not because it's true—but because you believe it's true! God created us so

that whatever we believe, we act on. Choose to believe what God says about you, and act accordingly. The Bible calls this *"the renewing of your mind"* (Romans 12:2).[15]

Prayer:

Lord, I surrender (CHILD'S NAME) into Your loving hands. Forgive (CHILD'S NAME) for focusing on negative thoughts. I ask that You fill (CHILD'S NAME)'s mind with things of the Holy Spirit that bring life and peace. Enable him/her to think positive and healthy thoughts. Help (CHILD'S NAME) to set (his/her) mind on the things of the Spirit (Romans 8:5). I pray that his/her thoughts and actions would line up with the truth of Your Word. Father, give (CHILD'S NAME) the grace to overcome negative thoughts and fix his/her mind with the things that are true, pure, and just (Philippians 4:8). Holy Spirit, please strip him/her of any self-inflicting thoughts and enable him/her to think thoughts that bring honor and glory to Your name. I pray that (CHILD'S NAME) will be transformed by the renewing of his/her mind (Romans 12:2a). Let the peace of God guard his/her heart and mind in Christ Jesus (Philippians 4:7). In Jesus's name, Amen!

Decree:

I declare and decree that every thought of (CHILD'S NAME) will come under the obedience of Jesus Christ

(2 Corinthians 10:5b). The enemy does not have authority over (CHILD'S NAME)'s mind; I deny all his access over (CHILD'S NAME)'s mind.

Additional Scripture References for a Sound Mind:

- *"And do not be conformed to this world, but be transformed by the renewing of your mind, that you may prove what is that good and acceptable and perfect will of God"* (Romans 12:2).
- *"Let this mind be in you which was also in Christ Jesus"* (Philippians 2:5).
- *"For the weapons of our warfare are not carnal but mighty in God for pulling down strongholds"* (2 Corinthians 10:4).
- *"For to set the mind on the flesh is death, but to set the mind of the Spirit is life and peace"* (Romans 8:6 ESV).

DAY 7

Prayer for Healing from Insecurity

Charm is deceitful, and beauty is passing, But a woman who fears the Lord, she shall be praised.

—Proverbs 31:30

Insecurity keeps many people from reaching their full potential. Satan's desire is to steal the secure identity from God's children. Without a secure identity, kids go to extreme measures to gain attention from others to feel good about themselves or withdraw into feelings of inadequacy, believing that they don't really matter. When they think they measure up, they become arrogant. When they assess that they don't measure up, they become depressed.

Insecurity is rooted in fear. The Word of God says that *"this world is fading away, along with everything that people crave"* (1 John 2:17a NLT). It is dangerous to gain our confidence from anything that perishes, including our appearance.

We will succeed in some areas of our lives and fail in others. These experiences are normal. Success or failure should not jeopardize one's self-worth. God is much less interested in our successes or failures than He is in our pursuit of a relationship with Him.[16]

Prayer:

Lord, we come to You and surrender (CHILD'S NAME) into Your hands. We thank and praise You that (CHILD'S NAME) is fearfully and wonderfully created in Your image (Psalm 139:14). You chose (CHILD'S NAME) before the foundations of the earth, and You have a divine purpose for his/her life (Ephesians 1:4a). When (CHILD'S NAME) struggles with insecurity, please remind him/her who he/she is in Christ. Lord, please help (CHILD'S NAME) find his/her identity in You. Your Word says that he/she is a new creation and that old things have passed away (2 Corinthians 5:17). Lord, we ask that You deliver (CHILD'S NAME) from any negative mindset that keeps him/her under bondage. Please cleanse (CHILD'S NAME) from anything that keeps him/her from becoming all You made him/her to be. Enable (CHILD'S NAME) to see himself/herself as a crown of glory in Your hands (Isaiah 62:3). Please remove all the unhealthy comparisons in (CHILD'S NAME) and help him/her to be confident in who he/she is in You. In Jesus's name, Amen!

Decree:

I declare and decree that (CHILD'S NAME) will be secure in God's love (Zephaniah 3:17b) and walk in the new identity that is found in Christ Jesus.

Additional Scripture References to Overcome Insecurity:

- *"Therefore, there is now no condemnation for those who are in Christ Jesus, because through Christ Jesus the law of the Spirit who gives life has set you free from the law of sin and death"* (Romans 8:1–2 NIV).
- *"He predestined us to adoption as sons and daughters through Jesus Christ to Himself, according to the good pleasure of His will"* (Ephesians 1:5 NASB).
- *"But you are a chosen generation, a royal priesthood, a holy nation, His own special people, that you may proclaim the praises of Him who called you out of darkness into His marvelous light"* (1 Peter 2:9).
- *"This means that anyone who belongs to Christ has become a new person. The old life is gone; a new life has begun"* (2 Corinthians 5:17 NLT)!

DAY 8

Prayer to Find Their "Identity" in Christ

I am the light of the world. Whoever follows me will never walk in darkness, but will have the light of life.

—John 8:12b NIV

When Jesus said, "I am the light of the world," he was defining himself. He was saying, "I know who I am." Over and over, he defined Himself. Jesus knew who He was, and as a result, He was not under pressure. This is the principle of identity. You discover who you are by knowing whose you are. The Bible says that you were created by God. He has a plan for your life.[17]

Identity confusion can persist in many aspects of one's life. "Virtually all adolescents wrestle with their sense of self-worth and consequently struggle with feelings of inferiority—even the brightest, prettiest, handsomest, and most gifted athletically."[18] McFarland offers additional insights:

> A healthy self-esteem isn't grounded in one's strengths or abilities. Teens cannot find their value by comparing themselves to others. Somebody will

always come along who is prettier, wealthier, smarter, or more athletic. That's inevitable. Our teens' self-esteem must come from the knowledge of who Jesus is and from the assurance of His love and care. Parents have the privilege of emphasizing these truths as they model acceptance, forgiveness, and love.[19]

Prayer:

Thank you, Father, for the plan and purpose You have for (CHILD'S NAME)'s life. Teach (CHILD'S NAME) how to embrace the plan You have for him/her (Jeremiah 29:11). Strengthen Your child and fill (him/her) with Your Spirit so that he/she may not walk according to the patterns of this world (Romans 12:2). I renounce the works of the enemy that would rob (CHILD'S NAME) of his/her God-given identity. Help (CHILD'S NAME) to understand that the world and its desires pass away. Be gracious to him/her to obey and fulfill Your Will in his/her life. (1 John 2:17). Lord, I praise You for being a God who is true and faithful in Your Word. Remind (CHILD'S NAME) that in Christ he/she is a new creation (2 Corinthians 5:17). Lord, help (CHILD'S NAME) not to define himself/herself as a loser, but to instead identify himself/herself as more than a conqueror in Christ Jesus (Romans 8:37). Empower (CHILD'S NAME) not to be swayed by the opinion of others, but to instead be confident in his/her identity in Christ.

Decree:

I declare and decree that (CHILD'S NAME) is God's workmanship created for His glory to proclaim His goodness (Ephesians 2:10).

Additional Scripture References to Find Their "Identity" in Christ:

- *"This means that anyone who belongs to Christ has become a new person. The old life is gone; a new life has begun"* (2 Corinthians 5:17 NLT)!
- *"Just as He chose us in Him before the foundation of the world, that we should be holy and without blame before Him in love"* (Ephesians 1:4).
- *"But you are a chosen generation, a royal priesthood, a holy nation, His own special people, that you may proclaim the praises of Him who called you out of darkness into His marvelous light"* (1 Peter 2:9).
- *"He predestined us to adoption as sons and daughters through Jesus Christ to Himself, according to the good pleasure of His will"* (Ephesians 1:5 NASB).

DAY 9

Prayer to Overcome Fear

When I am afraid, I put my trust in You.

—Psalm 56:3 NIV

Rick Warren shares these insights about how to overcome fear:

> Everyone has fears. Your problem isn't that you're afraid. It's what you do with the fear that really matters. Face your fears. Don't let them control you. Fear has an incredible ability to paralyze your potential. The closer you get to God, the more you're going to be filled with faith. The further away you get from God, the more you're going to be filled with fear.[20]

Billy Graham gives this advice: "Don't keep your secret fears welled up inside. Seek the Lord. Tell Him your fear. Ask for His help and have faith that He will come through. When you look to our great, big God, everything else gets smaller."[21] An old Irish proverb says, "Fear knocked at the door. Faith answered. There was no one there." Faith in God will help us overcome any fear in life. As we spend time in prayer and seek the Lord, He will deliver us from all fears (Psalm 34:4).

Prayer:

Father, I praise You and thank You that You are our stronghold in life. I thank You for the assurance that You are with us (Isaiah 43:5a). Lord, I submit (CHILD'S NAME) and all his/her fears into Your hands. I ask that You give (CHILD'S NAME) peace in place of those fears. (John 14:27). Enable (CHILD'S NAME) to choose faith over fear. I bind the spirit of fear that is tormenting (CHILD'S NAME)'s mind and ask that the Holy Spirit invade (CHILD'S NAME)'s heart and fill him/her with boldness and confidence. I renounce Satan and all his lies that would hold (CHILD'S NAME) in fear. I thank You that Your perfect love takes away all his/her fears (1 John 4:18). Father, please remove the fear of the future and instill in (CHILD'S NAME) a sense of hope. As Your Word says in Psalm 56:3, whenever (CHILD'S NAME) is afraid, please teach (CHILD'S NAME) to put his/her trust in You. In Jesus's name, Amen!

Decree:

I declare and decree that (CHILD'S NAME) will overcome fear and live a victorious life. Nothing causes (CHILD'S NAME) to be afraid because the Lord God is with (CHILD'S NAME) wherever he/she goes (Joshua 1:9b).

Additional Scripture References to Overcome Fear:

- *"For God has not given us a spirit of fear, but of power and of love and of a sound mind"* (2 Timothy 1:7).
- *"Be strong and of good courage, do not fear nor be afraid of them; for the Lord your God, He is the One who goes with you. He will not leave you nor forsake you"* (Deuteronomy 31:6).
- *"There is no fear in love; but perfect love casts out fear, because fear involves torment. But he who fears has not been made perfect in love"* (1 John 4:18).
- *"Fear not, for I am with you; Be not dismayed, for I am your God. I will strengthen you, Yes, I will help you, I will uphold you with My righteous right hand"* (Isaiah 41:10).

DAY 10

Prayer for Protection from the Enemy

Only by your power can we push back our enemies; only in your name can we trample our foes.

—Psalm 44:5 NLT

When the first plane hit the World Trade Center we thought it was accidental. When another plane hit it, we knew we were under attack. Today you are at war with the enemy. Only when you recognize that, victory is possible. When coming against spiritual forces, you must fight against spiritual weapons of the enemy. Never underestimate the power of the enemy. To fend off his attacks in your life and your family, you must be strong in the Lord.[22]

The Word of God says, *"Stay alert! Watch out for your great enemy, the devil. He prowls around like a roaring lion, looking for someone to devour"* (1 Peter 5:8 NLT).

Prayer:

Lord, I surrender (CHILD'S NAME) under Your feet. I thank You for all the times You've hidden (CHILD'S NAME) from the attack of the enemy. I praise You for the armor of God to protect us from the enemy (Ephesians 6:10–18). Father, I give You glory for sending Your Son Jesus Christ to destroy the works of the enemy (1 John 3:8b). I praise You that (CHILD'S NAME) is under the shadow of the Almighty (Psalm 91:1). Thank You for protecting (CHILD'S NAME) from hidden and unseen danger. Give (CHILD'S NAME) the grace to be strong because You are with him/her (Joshua 1:9). Deliver (CHILD'S NAME) from any evil power that tries to control his/her mind. Jesus, I stand on Your powerful Name and bind every evil influence that tries to invade (CHILD'S NAME)'s life through any means. Lord, I pray that You would keep (CHILD'S NAME) from all evil (Psalm 121:7). Cover (CHILD'S NAME) under Your precious Blood and protect him/her from any harm. In Jesus's name, Amen!

Decree:

I declare and decree that (CHILD'S NAME) is the son/daughter of the Most High. (CHILD'S NAME) will overcome the enemy by the blood of the Lamb and the word of His testimony (Revelation 12:11).

Additional Scripture References for Protection from the Enemy:

- *"Behold, I give you the authority to trample on serpents and scorpions, and over all the power of the enemy, and nothing shall by any means hurt you"* (Luke 10:19).

- *"Therefore submit to God. Resist the devil and he will flee from you"* (James 4:7).
- *"No weapon formed against you shall prosper"* (Isaiah 54:17a).
- "*For You have been a refuge for me, A tower of strength against the enemy*" (Psalm 61:3 NASB).

Part III

For Their Life at School and Work

DAY 11

Prayer to Reach Their Full God-given Potential

But each one has his own gift from God, one in this manner and another in that.

—1 Corinthians 7:7b

Talents, intelligence, musical ability, material possessions, cultural opportunities – everything is a gift from God. *"A man can only receive what is given to him from heaven"* (John 3:27b BSB). God never asks us to do more than we are capable of doing. But God expects us to live up to our potential and our privileges. You don't have to compete against anyone else. Don't compare yourself with others. You are only competing against yourself. You are only expected to do your best, not outperform someone else.[23]

Passivity is the neglect of our mind, time, gifts, or talents through inaction. God intends for us to cooperate actively with Him, but fear can have an immobilizing effect on our will. Passivity results in a dull life, avoiding risks, and missing opportunities.[24]

Prayer:

Dear Father, I come to You in Jesus's name and surrender (CHILD'S NAME)'s talents, gifts, and potential that You've entrusted to (him/her). Help (CHILD'S NAME) get a vision of his/her calling in life (2 Peter 1:10). Enable (CHILD'S NAME) to accomplish more than he/she ever dreamed of. I pray that (CHILD'S NAME) will develop and excel in the gifts and talents You've given him/her (Proverbs 22:29). Protect (CHILD'S NAME) from any plan of the enemy to steal away his/her God-given potential. Please guard his/her heart from jealousy, which leads to hating others' success. Lord, according to Your grace, enable (CHILD'S NAME) to use his/her gifts (1 Peter 4:10). If (CHILD'S NAME) has been passive in his/her work that led to any conflict, I pray for Your enabling grace to empower him/her to succeed in life. Please help (CHILD'S NAME) to rise to his/her level of greatness and use him/her for Your glory. I praise You that You will continue to work in (CHILD'S NAME) to use his/her potential to accomplish Your purpose on earth. In Jesus's name, Amen!

Decree:

I declare and decree that (CHILD'S NAME) will seize every chance to use his/her potential to serve God's purpose.

(CHILD'S NAME) can do all things through God Who strengthens him/her (Philippians 4:13).

Additional Scripture References to Reach Their God-given Potential:

- "Do you see a man *who* excels in his work? He will stand before kings; He will not stand before unknown *men*" (Proverbs 22:29).
- *"For we are God's masterpiece. He has created us anew in Christ Jesus, so we can do the good things he planned for us long ago"* (Ephesians 2:10 NLT).
- *"But you are a chosen generation, a royal priesthood, a holy nation, His own special people, that you may proclaim the praises of Him who called you out of darkness into His marvelous light"* (1 Peter 2:9).
- *"The LORD will hold you in his hand for all to see— a splendid crown in the hand of God."* (Isaiah 62:3 NLT)

DAY 12

Prayer for Wisdom

Wisdom is the principal thing; Therefore get wisdom. And in all your getting, get understanding.

—Proverbs 4:7

"Isaac D'Israel said, 'It is a wretched taste to be gratified with mediocrity when the excellence lies before us.' Excellence is the master key to success in any endeavor."[25]

The Word of God says, *"Blessed is the one who finds wisdom, and the one who gets understanding"* (Proverbs 3:13 ESV). Milton makes this observation:

The Lord offers wisdom freely; however, most don't bother to ask and, therefore, receive. Wisdom is, in fact, a divine gift that is granted by God whenever any believer asks. Wisdom is a spiritual act. It has very little to do with cognitive development. Wisdom does not come along with a sheepskin of a diploma or certification. Cry out to God, and He will answer you and anoint you with wisdom.[26]

Prayer:

Lord, I praise You, for You are the source of all wisdom. Your Divine wisdom is beyond our understanding. As Your Word teaches in Proverbs 2:2, please incline (CHILD'S NAME)'s ear to wisdom and his/her heart to understanding. According to Your Word, please instill reverential fear in (CHILD'S NAME) so that he/she may grow in wisdom (Proverbs 9:10). Increase a desire for knowledge and enlighten his/her understanding. Lord, You are a generous Father who gives wisdom without reproach as we ask for (CHILD'S NAME) (James 1:5). Lord, please give (CHILD'S NAME) Your words of wisdom so that the world shall not be able to refute or resist him/her (Luke 21:15). Father, deliver (CHILD'S NAME) from the thoughts of failure and give (him/her) a victorious mindset. Lord, Your Word says that Daniel was preferred above others because he had an excellent Spirit in him (Daniel 6:3). Please give Your Holy Spirit to (CHILD'S NAME) so that he/she will rise above mediocrity. In Jesus's name, Amen!

Decree:

I declare and decree that (CHILD'S NAME) will grow in the fear of the Lord and walk in wisdom (Proverbs 9:10a).

Additional Scripture References for Wisdom:

- *"The fear of the LORD is the beginning of wisdom; all those who practice it have a good understanding. His praise endures forever"* (Psalm 111:10 ESV)!
- *"If any of you lacks wisdom, you should ask God, who gives generously to all without finding fault, and it will be given to you"* (James 1:5 NIV).

- *"Blessed is the one who finds wisdom, and the one who gets understanding"* (Proverbs 3:13 ESV).
- *"How much better to get wisdom than gold! To get understanding is to be chosen rather than silver"* (Proverbs 16:16).

DAY 13

Prayer for Godly Friendship

A man who has friends must himself be friendly, But there is a friend who sticks closer than a brother.

—Proverbs 18:24

No one likes to feel alone and without a friend. We all recognize the importance of friendship and the priceless gift that a true friend can be. Deep friendship—the kind marked by consistency, honesty, and sensitivity—is the standard which the Bible holds up to us. A true friend is always loyal, regardless of circumstances. *"Faithful are the wounds of a friend"* (Proverbs 27:6a). Each of us is in need of friends who will hold us accountable when we err—and each of us is called to be that kind of friend, too.[27]

Friends should be chosen carefully because, as Paul told the Corinthians, *"Bad company corrupts good character"* (1 Corinthians 15:33b CEB). Godly friendships can strengthen one's spiritual life.

Prayer

Lord, I surrender (CHILD'S NAME) into Your hands and ask that You would bring godly friendship into his/her life. Guard (CHILD'S NAME) from comparison and covetousness. I pray that no thoughts of evil intention may enter their relationship. Lord, help (CHILD'S NAME) cultivate friendship with You as he/she spends time with You in prayer (John 15:15b). Give him/her grace to be connected with honest and faithful friends who speak the truth in love. As we read in Proverbs 13:20a, enable (CHILD'S NAME) to walk with wise friends to become wise. Please uproot any relationship in (CHILD'S NAME)'s life that is not of You. Father, please remove any habit of negative criticism and fault-finding in others and fill his/her heart with Your love (Matthew 7:1). Give (CHILD'S NAME) a heart of humility to accept his/her mistakes (Proverbs 28:13). Guide (CHILD'S NAME) to choose the right friendships that will encourage his/her faith and reflect Your love. In Jesus's name, Amen!

Decree:

I declare and decree that (CHILD'S NAME) will walk closely with God (Genesis 6:9b) and seek friendship that brings honor and glory to God.

Additional Scripture References for Godly Friendship:

- *"Do not be misled: "Bad company corrupts good character"* (1 Corinthians 15:33 NIV).

- *"As iron sharpens iron, so a friend sharpens a friend"* (Proverbs 27:17 NLT).
- *"A friend loves at all times"* (Proverbs 17:17a).
- *"Wise friends make you wise, but you hurt yourself by going around with fools"* (Proverbs 13:20 CEV).

DAY 14

Prayer for God's Favor

Let the favor of the Lord our God be upon us.

—Psalm 90:17 NASB 1995

Lord's favor is exceedingly great. It is unmerited and cannot be earned. It is given freely to the undeserving through faith in Christ and continues throughout our lives. There are people who work hard in an attempt to earn the favor of employers, parents, and friends. The acts of man will never earn God's favor, but He is pleased when we obey His commands with pure intentions. God's rich and abundant favor is readily available to all who will receive it by faith.[28]

We should seek favor for our children in prayer. A preacher reportedly said, "One day of favor is greater than a lifetime of labor."

Prayer:

Heavenly Father, in Jesus's name, I thank You for Who You are and for everything You've done in (CHILD'S NAME)'s life. I praise You for You have been so gracious to him/her. Lord, Your Word says that You will bless the righteous and surround them with favor as with a shield

(Psalm 5:12b). Therefore, Father, I am standing on Your promise that You will surround (CHILD'S NAME) with favor as with a shield. And I ask that the favor You have given (CHILD'S NAME) would increase daily. I seek Your favor for (CHILD'S NAME)'s life. Be gracious and merciful to (CHILD'S NAME) according to Your promise (Psalm 119:58). Lord, as Your Word says in Psalm 84:11, bestow favor upon (CHILD'S NAME) and give him/her grace to walk blameless in Your sight. I pray that by Your Divine favor, every door of opportunity would open for (CHILD'S NAME). Please impact every area of (CHILD'S NAME)'s life by Your grace and favor. In Jesus's name, Amen!!

Decree:

Father, in Jesus's name, I declare and decree that favor will be released in (CHILD'S NAME) today. I declare that (CHILD'S NAME) will have favor with God and man (Luke 2:52).

Additional Scripture References for God's Favor:

- *"For those who find me (wisdom) find life and receive favor from the Lord"* (Proverbs 8:35 NIV).
- *"Good people obtain favor from the Lord"* (Proverbs 12:2a NIV).

- *"Let the favor of the Lord our God be upon us; And confirm for us the work of our hands; Yes, confirm the work of our hands"* (Psalm 90:17 NASB 1995).
- *"For the Lord God is a sun and shield; the Lord bestows favor and honor; no good thing does he withhold from those whose walk is blameless"* (Psalm 84:11 NIV).

DAY 15

Prayer for Protection from Indoctrination in School

For we are not ignorant of his schemes.

—2 Corinthians 2:11b NASB

One of Satan's devices is to present the bait and hide the hook; to present the golden cup and hide the poison; to present the sweet, the pleasure, and the profit that may flow in upon the soul by yielding to sin—and by hiding from the soul the wrath and misery that will certainly follow the committing of sin. By this device he deceived our first parents. And so, it is that this same device of temptation continues today with the increase in the indoctrination of children in the culture of our time. Christian parents must entrench themselves in core Biblical principles and fundamental Biblical convictions so that they may embrace their God-given duty to guide their children against these indoctrinations.[29]

Be aware of the forces at school that seek to reshape the beliefs of your children. Stay attuned to what the children are being taught. Go into your children's bedrooms at night and pray over them as they sleep. Only God can perfectly protect your children against the attacks of Satan, and this fallen world.[30]

Prayer:

Father, we praise You, for You are the good Shepherd and teacher. In Jesus's name, we come against the evil scheme to lead (CHILD'S NAME) into gender confusion and indoctrination in school. God, You have given us authority over (CHILD'S NAME). As we read in Proverbs 22:6, help us to train and teach (CHILD'S NAME) in the way he/she should go. Enable us not to give up that God-given right to anyone who tries to harm (CHILD'S NAME). We come against the plan that eradicates the concept of right and wrong in his/her life. Holy Spirit, fill us with righteous anger to stand against the gender ideology and pronouns that try to rob (CHILD'S NAME) of his/her God-given identity and confuse their mind. If (CHILD'S NAME) has believed any ideology that is contrary to the truth, we speak healing over his/her mind. Give him/her diligence in following Your commands (Deuteronomy 6:17) and be confident in who he/she is created to be. Please protect (CHILD'S NAME) from being exposed to harmful and perverse content. I thank You that You are faithful to guard (CHILD'S NAME) against the evil one (2 Thessalonians 3:3). Through Christ, we have been given all authority over all the power of the enemy (Luke 10:19). We rely on Your Word and bind up the plan of the enemy in Jesus's name, Amen!

Decree:

I declare and decree that God's presence would guard and protect (CHILD'S NAME). He/She will hear the voice of the Good Shepherd and follow only His ways (John 10:27).

Additional Scripture References to Protect Children from Indoctrination in School:

- *"Woe to those who call evil good and good evil, who put darkness for light and light for darkness, who put bitter for sweet and sweet for bitter"* (Isaiah 5:20 NIV).
- *"So that no advantage would be taken of us by Satan, for we are not ignorant of his schemes"* (2 Corinthians 2:11 NASB).
- *"And you shall teach them diligently to your children and speak of them when you sit at home and when you walk along the road, when you lie down and when you get up"* (Deuteronomy 6:7 BSB).
- *"Do not be carried away by all kinds of strange teachings. It is good for our hearts to be strengthened by grace"* (Hebrews 13:9a NIV).

Part IV

For Their Commitment to God

DAY 16

Prayer for Salvation

For the Son of Man came to seek and to save the lost.

—Luke 19:10 NIV

Prayer releases power from the Holy Spirit, which brings about the new birth or salvation. Decreeing God's Word and speaking forth Spirit-led declarations are two of the ways we release the birthing power of the Holy Spirit. They do not release Him in the sense that he is bound—God obviously is not bound. But His creative power, energy and ability that come forth through His Word are released upon the earth as we speak them for Him. We are His partners, His representatives.[31]

Trust in the Holy Spirit to work in your child's heart.

Prayer:

Lord, I thank You for the power of Your Salvation. I line up my prayers with Your Word according to Your will for (CHILD'S

NAME)'s life. Lord, I depend on Your Word (Acts 26:18a) and ask that You would open (CHILD'S NAME)'s eyes and turn him/her from darkness to light—from the power of Satan to God—so that he/she may receive forgiveness of sins. I pray that (CHILD'S NAME) would confess with his/her mouth that Jesus is Lord and that he/she would believe in his/her heart that you have raised Christ from the dead (Romans 10:9). God, please give (CHILD'S NAME) a heart to call on Your name and be saved (Romans 10:13). Lord, please remove the heart of stone from (CHILD'S NAME) and give him/her a tender and responsive heart (Ezekiel 36:26). I rely on Your grace that brings salvation in (CHILD'S NAME) life through faith (Ephesians 2:8). Give (CHILD'S NAME) an undivided heart and cause (CHILD'S NAME) to walk in Your ways (Ezekiel 11:19). Lord, I pray for (CHILD'S NAME) that You would grant him/her repentance that leads to the knowledge of Your truth (2 Timothy 2:25). I praise You Jesus for the power in Your name that leads (CHILD'S NAME) to salvation (Acts 4:12). In Jesus's name, Amen!

Decree:

I declare and decree that all my children will be taught by the Lord (Isaiah 54:13) and come to the knowledge of God through His saving grace.

Additional Scripture References for Salvation:

- *"God saved you by his grace when you believed. And you can't take credit for this; it is a gift from God"* Ephesians 2:8 (NLT).
- *"If you openly declare that Jesus is Lord and believe in your heart that God raised him from the dead, you will be saved"* (Romans 10:9 NLT).
- *"He saved us, not because of the righteous things we had done, but because of his mercy. He washed away our sins, giving us a new birth and new life through the Holy Spirit"* (Titus 3:5 NLT).
- *"If anyone is in Christ* [that is, grafted in, joined to Him by faith in Him as Savior], *he is a new creature* [reborn and renewed by the Holy Spirit]*; the old things* [the previous moral and spiritual condition] *have passed away. Behold, new things have come* [because spiritual awakening brings a new life]" (2 Corinthians 5:17 AMP).

DAY 17

Prayer for "Fear of the Lord"

Blessed is everyone who fears the Lord.

—Psalm 128:1a ESV

The fear of God doesn't mean shrinking in fear before Him. A. W. Tozer says, "The greatness of God rouses fear within us, but His goodness encourages us not to be afraid of Him. To fear and not to be afraid—that is the paradox of faith."[32] Missler offers additional clarification of what the fear of the Lord means:

Fear of God is caring more about what God thinks than about what we think. It means to stand in reverential awe of who God is and to hate sin. We cannot stand reverentially in who God is until we really know Him and have an intimate relationship with Him. We cannot know Him unless we hate sin.[33]

Oswald Chambers says, "The remarkable thing about fearing God is that when you fear God you fear nothing else, whereas, if you do not fear God, you fear everything else."[34]

Prayer:

Lord, I stand in awe of Your name. Your name is Holy, and You are worthy to be praised. I thank You for the abundant mercy and grace You have extended in (CHILD'S NAME)'s life. I surrender (CHILD'S NAME) into Your hands. Lord, according to Your Word, give him/her a heart to fear You and hate evil (Proverbs 8:13a). Remove any ungodly fear that controls (CHILD'S NAME)'s heart and impart in him/her godly fear that enables him/her to depart from evil. Lord, instill in (CHILD'S NAME) a reverential fear that fulfills his/her desires and delivers him/her from harm (Psalm 145:19). Remove from (CHILD'S NAME) the fear of man and replace it with godly fear that leads to life (Proverbs 19:23). Lord, Your Word says, *"The fear of the Lord is the beginning of wisdom"* (Proverbs 9:10a). Please help (CHILD'S NAME) to seek the fear of the Lord that leads to wisdom. I pray that godly fear would direct him/her toward righteous living before Your presence. In Jesus's name , Amen!

Decree:

I declare and decree that the fear of the Lord in (CHILD'S NAME) will lead to riches, honor, and life (Proverbs 22:4).

Additional Scripture References for Fear of the Lord:

- *"Fear the Lord, you His godly people, for those who fear him will have all they need"* (Psalm 34:9 NLT).

- *"The Lord is my light and my salvation; whom shall I fear? The Lord is the strength of my life; of whom shall I be afraid"* (Psalm 27:1)?
- *"Be not wise in your own eyes; fear the Lord and turn away from evil"* (Proverbs 3:7 ESV).
- *"In the fear of the Lord there is strong confidence, and His children will have a place of refuge"* (Proverbs 14:26).

DAY 18

Prayer to Love God's Word

For the word of God is living and powerful.

—Hebrews 4:12a

The Word of God is a great help in prayer. A reverence for God's Holy Name is closely related to a high regard for His Word. Jesus was a man of prayer, and he magnified the Word of God, quoting often from the Scriptures. No man loves the Bible, who does not love to pray. No man loves to pray who does not delight in His Word.[35]

The Word of God is not a trifle; it is a matter of life and death. If you treat the Scriptures as a trifle or as empty words, you forfeit life. Even our physical life depends on God's word, because by His word, we were created (Hebrews 11:3). Our spiritual life begins by the word of God (1 Peter 1:23).[36]

The Word of God has the power to heal and deliver. *"He sent His word and healed them and delivered them from their destruction"* (Psalm 107:20). The prophet Jeremiah ate the Word of God, and it became the joy and rejoicing of his heart (Jeremiah 15:16a). That is what the Word of God does when we dwell on it. A. W. Tozer says that "Satan's greatest weapon is man's ignorance of God's Word."[37]

Prayer:

Lord, we praise You and thank You for Your Word, which is living and powerful (Hebrews 4:12). We trust in Your Word, for it never passes away (Matthew 24:35). Father, please sanctify (CHILD'S NAME) by Your Word of truth (John 17:17). We come before You and ask that by the power of Your Word, You would touch his/her heart, will, thoughts, and emotions. Help (CHILD'S NAME) to be willing to obey Your Word. By the power of Your Word, let every chain of unbelief and disobedience be broken in (CHILD'S NAME)'s life. Lord, enable (CHILD'S NAME) to stay pure and live according to Your Word (Psalm 119:9). Father, teach (CHILD'S NAME) to hide Your Word in his/her heart, so that he/she might not sin against You (Psalm 119:11). Remove any regrets from his/her soul and strengthen him/her according to Your Word (Psalm 119:28). Please speak to (CHILD'S NAME) every time he/she reads Your Word. Plant Your Word in (CHILD'S NAME)'s heart and increase his/her faith according to Your Word (Romans 10:17). Let Your Word become a source of guidance for (CHILD'S NAME) life (Psalm 119:105). Father, give (CHILD'S NAME) strength and resolution to meditate on the Word of God, and obey Your Word, which brings (him/her) success in life (Joshua 1:8). In Jesus's name, Amen!

Decree:

I declare and decree that (CHILD'S NAME) will overcome the enemy's attack by the power of God's Word (Matthew 4: 3–10).

Additional Scripture References to Love God's Word:

- *"My Word . . . shall accomplish what I please, And it shall prosper in the thing for which I sent it"* (Isaiah 55:11b).
- *"Let the word of Christ dwell in you richly in all wisdom, teaching and admonishing one another in psalms and hymns and spiritual songs, singing with grace in your hearts to the Lord"* (Colossians 3:16).
- *"All Scripture is given by inspiration of God, and is profitable for doctrine, for reproof, for correction, for instruction in righteousness"* (2 Timothy 3:16).
- *"As for God, His way is blameless; The word of the LORD is refined; He is a shield to all who take refuge in Him"* (2 Samuel 22:31 NASB).

Part V

For Their Spiritual Growth

DAY 19

Prayer for Healthy Emotions

Don't sin by letting anger control you. Don't let the sun go down while you are still angry.

—Ephesians 4:26 NLT

Michael Houdman says, "We must be mindful of the things we think about, the things we set our affection on, and the things we give our attention to. Negativity, bitterness, and anger can take root in our hearts and lead to sinful behavior."[38] With God's help, we can learn to manage every negative emotion by the power of the Holy Spirit.

According to Galatians 5:22–23, the Holy Spirit produces fruit that is pleasing to God. The fruit of the Spirit is love, joy, peace, patience, kindness, goodness, faithfulness, gentleness, and self-control. (Instead of hate, sorrow, anxiety, anger, harshness, hard feelings, insincerity, hardness, and passions)

The heart is the source of all emotions; *"for everything you do flows from it"* (Proverbs 4:23b NIV).

Prayer:

Lord, I thank you for all the blessings that You have showered in (CHILD'S NAME)'s life. Enable (CHILD'S NAME) to forsake all anger in his/her life (Psalm 37:8) and not give place to it for even a moment. Help (CHILD'S NAME) to be quick to forgive and not to hold a grudge toward anyone. Lord, give him/her the grace to never give place to jealousy in any way (Proverbs 14:30). Empower (CHILD'S NAME) to be so filled with the fruit of the Spirit that envy never enters (CHILD'S NAME)'s heart or mind. Just as Your Word promises in James 1:4, strengthen (CHILD'S NAME) to choose to have patience in all things so that he/she can be complete and whole, lacking nothing. Lord, please give (CHILD'S NAME) a compassionate, loving, and patient heart toward others so that (CHILD'S NAME) is not tempted to show anger toward anyone. Lord, quicken the heart of (CHILD'S NAME) with the strength of the Holy Spirit to take control of his/her emotions and rise above anxiety or depression. Father, according to Your Word, help (CHILD'S NAME) fix his/her mind on the things of the Spirit to experience life and peace (Romans 8:6). In Jesus's name, Amen!

Decree:

I declare and decree that the peace of God, which surpasses all understanding will guard (CHILD'S NAME)'s heart and mind in Christ Jesus (Philippians 4:7).

Additional Scripture References for Healthy Emotions:

- *"You will keep in perfect peace all who trust in you, all whose thoughts are fixed on you"* (Isaiah 26:3 NLT)!
- *"Better a patient person than a warrior, one with self-control than one who takes a city.* (Proverbs 16:32 NIV).
- *"Anxiety in the heart of man causes depression, But a good word makes it glad"* (Proverbs 12:25).
- *"For where envy and self-seeking exist, confusion and every evil thing are there"* (James 3:16).

DAY 20

Prayer for Faith in God

Now faith is the substance of things hoped for, the evidence of things not seen.

—Hebrews 11:1

Everyone has faith at some level in something. God has given us a *"measure of faith"* (Romans 12:3). We need the right kind of faith. Faith is confident trust.

Measure your faith by the degree to which you are not overcome by circumstances around you, not being discouraged by the forces against you, and not being conformed to the world around you. Measure your life by the blessed assurance you have that God is in charge of your present and your future, your circumstances, and all that touches your life. Measure your faith by the unwavering confidence that God is your Father and that He can work all things for His glory and your good (Romans 8:28). The more you trust God, the more the atmosphere around will change.[39]

The Word of God is the source of our faith. John the Apostle said, *"This is the victory that has overcome the world, even our faith"* (1 John 5:4b NIV).

Prayer:

Lord, I praise You for *"You are the author and finisher of our faith"* (Hebrews 12:2a). Please fill (CHILD'S NAME) with the spirit of faith that he/she would live to please You in everything (Hebrews 11:6). Lord, Your Word says that faith comes by hearing and hearing by the Word of God (Romans 10:17). Increase the level of faith in (CHILD'S NAME) as he/she reads and meditates upon Your Word. Lord, by Your grace, enable (CHILD'S NAME) to stand fast in faith in times of doubt. Lord, You have said that the just shall live by faith (Romans 1:17). Help (CHILD'S NAME) to always live by faith. Father, please give him/her boldness to approach Your throne by faith (Ephesians 3:12). Let (CHILD'S NAME)'s faith be evident in his/her prayer life. Empower him/her to hold onto faith in tough times. By faith help (CHILD'S NAME) to overcome the world and achieve victory in life (1 John 5:4). In Jesus's name, Amen!

Decree:

I declare and decree that, according to God's Word, (CHILD'S NAME) will achieve the impossible by his/her faith (Mark 9:23).

Additional Scripture References for faith in God:

- *"And whatever you ask in prayer, you will receive, if you have faith"* (Matthew 21:22 ESV).

- *"Now faith is confidence in what we hope for and assurance about what we do not see"* (Hebrews 11:1 NIV).
- *"That your faith should not be in the wisdom of men but in the power of God"* (1 Corinthians 2:5).
- *"For we live by faith, not by sight"* (2 Corinthians 5:7 NIV).

DAY 21

Prayer for Righteous Living

For all have sinned and fall short of the glory of God.

—Romans 3:23

Anyone who thinks of himself as a pretty good person ought to think again. We came into this world spiritually dead—ruled by Satan, his world system, and our sinful nature. From the divine perspective, we deserve punishment. God is so Holy that He is separated from all sin. Everything He does is right, and by comparison, even mankind's righteous acts are like filthy rags.[40]

Isaiah says, *"And all our righteousnesses are like filthy rags"* (Isaiah 64:6b). But if we confess our sins, God will forgive our sins and make us righteous (1 John 1:9). God answers our prayers in His righteousness (Psalm 143:1). It is in Christ that we are a new creation (2 Corinthians 5:17).

Prayer:

Lord, Your Word says that no human being is good before You (Psalm 53:3). Father, we are grateful that Your blood that was shed on the cross cleanses our sins and makes us righteous.

I humbly come before You and surrender (CHILD'S NAME) into Your hands. Help him/her to acknowledge that his/her salvation is not a result of his/her works. Father, according to Your Word, let the righteousness of God be manifested in (CHILD'S NAME)'s life by his/her faith in Jesus Christ (Romans 3:21). Father, You demonstrated Your righteousness in the crucifixion of Your Son (Romans 3:25a). Lord, let this truth be deposited in (CHILD'S NAME) so that he/she will never take credit for any of his/her good works. Help (CHILD'S NAME) to understand that he/she is justified by faith, not by his/her righteousness (Romans 3:27–28). Lord, I thank You that You made Christ sin on behalf of (CHILD'S NAME) so that he/she might become the righteousness of God (2 Corinthians 5:21).

Decree:

I declare and decree that God's righteousness will reign in (CHILD'S NAME)'s life through Jesus Christ (Romans 5:17b).

Additional Scripture References for Righteousness:

- *"God made him who had no sin to be sin for us, so that in him we might become the righteousness of God"* (2 Corinthians 5:21 NIV).
- *"Save me from the guilt of bloodshed, God, the God of my salvation; Then my tongue will joyfully sing of Your righteousness"* (Psalm 51:14 NASB).

- *"I bring near My righteousness; it is not far off; And My salvation will not delay"* (Isaiah 46:13a ESV).
- *"If you know that He is righteous, you may be sure that everyone who practices righteousness has been born of Him"* (1 John 2:29 ESV).

DAY 22

Prayer for the Work of the Holy Spirit

If you then, being evil, know how to give good gifts to your children, how much more will your heavenly Father give the Holy Spirit to those who ask Him!

—Luke 11:13

The Holy Spirit is the presence of God in our life. The truth is, if we cannot pray for the Holy Spirit, we cannot pray for any good thing, for He is the sum of all good to us. The Holy Spirit helps us in prayer. The ability of God to answer and work through our prayers is measured by the Divine energy that God has been enabled to put in us by the Holy Spirit. The projecting power of praying is the measure of the Holy Spirit in us. Ask for the Holy Spirit-seek for the Holy Spirit-knock for the Holy Spirit. He is the Father's greatest gift for the child's greatest need.[41]

Prayer:

Father, we come before Your presence and worship You. Thank You for the Holy Spirit promised to Your Children in the last days (Joel 2:28a). Lord, according to Your Word, we ask that You would give the Holy Spirit to (CHILD'S NAME). We pray that the Spirit of truth would invade (CHILD'S NAME)'s life and guide him/her into all the truth (John 16:13a). God, pour out Your love into (CHILD'S NAME)'s heart through the power of Your Holy Spirit (Romans 5:5). Father, according to Your will, please impart the gifts of the Holy Spirit in (CHILD'S NAME) (Hebrews 2:4). We pray the Helper, the Holy Spirit, will abide in (CHILD'S NAME) forever (John 14:16). Lord, give grace to (CHILD'S NAME) so that he/she will not grieve the Holy Spirit of God by willful sin or rebellion (Isaiah 63:10a). Breathe Your breath upon every area of his/her life. We give You total control over (CHILD'S NAME)'s life. Lead him/her to a life of freedom, for where the Spirit of the Lord is, there is freedom (2 Corinthians 3:17). Please fill (CHILD'S NAME) with the Spirit of prayer so that he/she will be able to pray according to the will of God (Romans 8:26–27). In Jesus's name, Amen!

Decree:

I declare and decree that the prayer of (CHILD'S NAME) is powerful and effective (James 5:16b). The power of the Holy Spirit will be evident in (CHILD'S NAME)'s life!

Additional Scripture References for the Work of the Holy Spirit:

- *"And do not grieve the Holy Spirit of God, with whom you were sealed for the day of redemption"* (Ephesians 4:30 NIV).
- *"And I will ask the Father, and he will give you another Helper, to be with you forever"* (John 14:16 ESV).
- *"Now hope does not disappoint, because the love of God has been poured out in our hearts by the Holy Spirit who was given to us"* (Romans 5:5).
- *"Do you not know that you are the temple of God and that the Spirit of God dwells in you"* (1 Corinthians 3:16)?

DAY 23

Prayer for Their "Walk with God"

Can two people walk together without agreeing on the direction?

—Amos 3:3 NLT

The Prophet Jeremiah says that *"no one who walks determines his own steps"* (Jeremiah 10:23b HCSB). Unless our walk is directed by God, it will be without purpose.

How do we walk with God every day? We do it the same way we strengthen our relationship with a friend, or with our spouse: we spend time with them—talking and listening to each other. We "walk" with them enjoying their company and sharing our lives. The same is true with God.[42] God desires that we become more dependent upon Him every step of our way. God desires us to walk humbly with Him (Micah 6:8).

Tony Evans explains:

> The Bible says that Enoch walked with God (Genesis 5:24). Enoch was walking with God while the rest of the society was walking with idols. Most of the people around him were out of step with God. It

didn't bother Enoch to be out of step with everything and everyone else because he had a rich fellowship with God—a relationship that was passionate and powerful. He wouldn't have traded that for anything else.[43] Walking with God is a choice.

Prayer:

Lord, I pray that (CHILD'S NAME) would enjoy a close relationship with You. Give (CHILD'S NAME) Your grace to be in agreement with You for Your will in his/her life (Amos 3:3). Father, take the lead in every decision that (CHILD'S NAME) makes. God of the universe, walking with You sometimes requires (CHILD'S NAME) to stay away from many things of this world. Please give him/her the strength to depend on Your grace. Lord, help (CHILD'S NAME) to wrestle in prayer just like Jacob until he/she gets an answer from You (Genesis 32:22-32). Father, I pray that (CHILD'S NAME) would be able to hear Your voice saying, *"This is the way, walk in it"* whether he/she turns to the right or the left (Isaiah 30:21). Please give (CHILD'S NAME) a desire to walk faithfully with You, just like Enoch, and live blameless in Your sight (Genesis 5:24). In Jesus's name, Amen!

Decree:

I declare and decree that (CHILD'S NAME) will have a desire to have a close relationship with God and walk in the light as He walked (1 John 1:7).

Additional Scripture References for their Walk with God:

- *"Guide my steps by Your Word, so I will not be overcome by evil"* (Psalm 119:133 NLT).
- *"My steps have stayed on your path; I have not wavered from following you"* (Psalm 17:5 NLT).
- *"I will instruct you and teach you in the way you should go; I will guide you with My eye"* (Psalm 32:8).
- *"Our heart has not turned back, nor have our steps departed from Your way"* (Psalm 44:18 ESV).

Part VI

For Their Deliverance

DAY 24

Prayer for Deliverance from Manipulative and Controlling Spirits

Most assuredly, I say to you, whoever commits sin is a slave of sin.

—John 8:34b

We've all known manipulative people, whether they are friends, children, or our spouse. They might scare, coerce, obligate, criticize, guilt trip, bribe, blame, undermine, and intimidate. Or they flatter, offer sympathy, and act innocent—but not with sincerity. It's all emotional blackmail. It's manipulation. In short, manipulation is a counterfeit way of getting our needs met.[44]

"For where jealousy and selfish ambition exist, there will be disorder and every vile practice" (James 3:16 ESV). Manipulation is a form of lying. Satan is the father of lies (John 8:44b).

The spirit of manipulation and control may influence some children to rebel against their parents; we must watch out for this spirit in our lives. It will destroy our relationships and rob us of our peace; we must rebuke this spirit and depend on God's grace to overcome it.

Prayer

Dear Father, we [parents] come before Your throne of mercy and ask Your forgiveness if we have allowed this manipulating Spirit to control our relationship in any way. Cleanse us from all unrighteousness.

Lord, we pray for (CHILD'S NAME) that he/she would have a conviction through the help of the Holy Spirit to turn away from manipulative and controlling tactics. We acknowledge that it is not in (CHILD'S NAME) to direct his/her steps (Jeremiah 10:23). We surrender (CHILD'S NAME) into Your hands and ask that You would set him/her free from the unhealthy desire to manipulate and control others. We bind the spirit of deception and lies that tries to control (CHILD'S NAME)'s life to have his/her way.

Lord, we apply the blood of Jesus Christ on (CHILD'S NAME)'s heart and mind. We rebuke all the spirits of control that try to manipulate others to have his/her way. Lord, Your Word says, *"If two of you agree on earth concerning anything that they ask, it will be done for them by My Father in heaven"* (Matthew 18:19). We come in agreement and ask that You would deliver (CHILD'S NAME) from all spirits that try to manipulate and control others. Sovereign Lord, we release (CHILD'S NAME) into Your hands. Please take control of (CHILD'S NAME)'s life and give him/her a heart that is willing to yield to Your Spirit. In Jesus's name, Amen!

Decree:

I declare and decree that (CHILD'S NAME) will excel in showing respect for others (Romans 12:10b). The spirit that controlled (CHILD'S NAME) is broken in the name of Jesus and by the power of the Holy Spirit.

Additional Scripture References to overcome Manipulative and Controlling Spirit:

- *"I know, O Lord, that a man's way is not his own; no one who walks directs his own steps"* (Jeremiah 10:23 BSB).
- *"My friends, you were chosen to be free. So don't use your freedom as an excuse to do anything you want. Use it as an opportunity to serve each other with love"* (Galatians 5:13 CEV).
- *"Be as shrewd as snakes and as innocent as doves"* (Matthew 10:16b NIV).
- *"When He, the Spirit of truth, comes, He will guide you into all the truth"* (John 16:13a NASB).

DAY 25

Prayer for Freedom from Addiction to Social Media

For the flesh desires what is contrary to the Spirit, and the Spirit what is contrary to the flesh. They are in conflict with each other, so that you are not to do whatever you want.

—Galatians 5:17 NIV

The technology that promises to release us from boredom is actually making it worse—making us more prone to seek empty distractions than we have ever been. The more you entertain children, the more bored they will get. The problem, as with so many short-term solutions, is that solving the immediate problem requires leaving a bigger problem unsolved—and actually makes the bigger problem worse.[45]

Researchers believe that as teens become hooked on social media apps, they are less able to regulate emotions, manage impulses, and make good decisions. Social media addiction also creates lower self-esteem. When our teens spend an excessive amount of time online, they are on a journey to find their identity by comparing themselves to others. The fame, beauty, wit, status, and identity of other online teens become the measuring stick by which they judge their value. They can never measure up; they are susceptible to anxiety and depression.[46]

Whatever may be the addiction, do not lose hope.

Prayer:

Father, we are so grateful that You are the Sovereign Lord and that nothing is too hard for You (Jeremiah 32:17). We confess our inability to control or help (CHILD'S NAME) in this addiction. Lord, Your Word says that we deceive ourselves if we claim to be without sin (1 John 1:8). We ask that You would instill Your truth in (CHILD'S NAME) to accept the struggle with this issue. Please forgive (CHILD'S NAME) all his/her sins and cleanse him/her from all unrighteousness. Father, we pray that social media will not influence his/her life but that their life would be built upon real experience. Please protect (CHILD'S NAME)'s mind from any harmful content online before he/she even sees it. Put a hedge of protection around him/her (Job 1:10a). Lord, Your Word says that a person without self-control is like a city with broken-down walls (Proverbs 25:28).

By the enabling power of the Holy Spirit, we ask that You help (CHILD'S NAME) to overcome this addiction. Father, we confess that other lords besides You have ruled over (CHILD'S NAME) (Isaiah 26:13). But we rely on Your mighty name, which can deliver (CHILD'S NAME) from this addiction. We acknowledge that the mighty power that comes from the Holy Spirit can help (CHILD'S NAME) to overcome this. Please restore in (CHILD'S NAME) a desire for what is good and teach him/her to depend on You. In Jesus's name, Amen!

Decree:

I declare and decree that the anointing of the Holy Spirit will break the chains of bondage in (CHILD'S NAME) and he/she will live and walk in freedom all the days of his/her life (Isaiah 10:27b).

Additional Scripture References for freedom from Social Media Addiction:

- *"For sin will no longer be a master over you, since you are not under Law* [as slaves], *but under* [unmerited] *grace* [as recipients of God's favor and mercy]" (Romans 6:14 AMP).
- *"Some of you were once like that. But you were cleansed; you were made holy; you were made right with God by calling on the name of the Lord Jesus Christ and by the Spirit of our God"* (1 Corinthians 6:11 NLT).
- *"Clothe yourself with the presence of the Lord Jesus Christ. And don't let yourself think about ways to indulge your evil desires"* (Romans 13:14 NLT).
- *"For you did not receive the spirit of bondage again to fear, but you received the Spirit of adoption by whom we cry out, 'Abba, Father'"* (Romans 8:15).

DAY 26

Prayer to Break Every Chain from Demonic Influences

Our struggle is not against flesh and blood, but against the rulers, against the powers, against the world forces of this darkness, against the spiritual forces of wickedness in the heavenly places.

—Ephesians 6:12 NASB

Most people of all age groups are deceived and living defeated in many areas of life. Our heavenly Father desires all of us to walk in freedom. Many children and young adults are drawn toward playing on the Ouija board, Tarot cards, palm reading, and similar activities. "The main use of these games is for divination purposes. It is evil. All forms of divination, no matter how seemingly harmless, can potentially open someone up to much deeper problems, such as direct demonic oppression, obsession, and possession."[47]

Some kids invite evil into their lives by watching horror and haunting shows, listening to filthy music, and reading materials that quench their thirst for our God. Satan's first and foremost strategy is to deceive people. He deceives the whole world (Revelation 12:9b), and the whole world is under the control of the evil one (1 John 5:19).

Reading God's Word with the help of the Holy Spirit enables one to understand more about God things and to make the right judgments about all things (1 Corinthians 2:11b and 15a). The name of Jesus, His blood shed on the cross for the forgiveness of sins, His living Word, and the Holy Spirit Anointing have the power to break every chain and demonic influence in one's life and set them free.

Prayer:

Lord, I surrender (CHILD'S NAME) into Your loving hands. I plead the blood of Jesus Christ over his/her body, soul, spirit, will, mind, feelings, and emotions. Jesus, I thank You that You bore our sins on the cross (1 Peter 2:24). Please forgive (CHILD'S NAME) of any sin that opened the door for any demonic influence in his/her life and cleanse him/her from all unrighteousness. Make (CHILD'S NAME) dead to the power of sin and alive in Christ (Romans 6:11). Help him/her to understand that a deck of cards cannot predict one's future. Lord, Your Word says that the law of the Spirit of life in Christ Jesus has set you free from the law of sin and of death (Romans 8:2). I confess that the power of the demonic influence over (CHILD'S NAME)'s life is broken by the powerful name of Jesus. Lord, Your Word says that where the Spirit of the Lord is, there is freedom (2 Corinthians 3:17). Please fill (CHILD'S NAME) with the power of the Holy

Spirit and set him/her free from any demonic influence. Lord, Your Word says there is a spirit that works in the children of disobedience (Ephesians 2:2b). If there is any persistent rebellion or disobedience in (CHILD'S NAME)'s life, please deliver him/her from such a spirit and help him/her walk in freedom. By the authority in Jesus's name, I command that evil spirit to come out of (CHILD'S NAME) and never enter him/her again (Mark 9:25b). Lord, let the life in Your Word bring healing in (CHILD'S NAME)'s life (Psalm 107:20a). Lord, I ask that You would give (CHILD'S NAME) a right mind and strengthen him/her to stand firm and not to submit again to a yoke of slavery (Galatians 5:1). In Jesus's name, Amen!

Decree:

I declare and decree that He who is in (CHILD'S NAME) is greater than he who is in the world and Satan has no power over (CHILD'S NAME)'s life (1 John 4:4). He/She is more than a conqueror through Christ Jesus (Romans 8:37).

Additional Scripture References to Break Free from Demonic Influences:

- *"For he has rescued us from the dominion of darkness and brought us into the kingdom of the Son he loves"* (Colossians 1:13 NIV).

- *"In Him you have been made complete, and He is the head over all rule and authority"* (Colossians 2:10 NASB 1995).
- *"He . . . disarmed the rulers and authorities, He made a public display of them, having triumphed over them through Him"* (Colossians 2:15 NASB).
- *"How can anyone enter the strong man's house and carry off his property, unless he first binds the strong man"* (Matthew 12:29a NASB 1995)?

DAY 27

Prayer for Freedom from Addiction and All Kinds of Spirits

Truly I tell you, whatever you bind on earth will be bound in heaven, and whatever you loose on earth will be loosed in heaven.

—Matthew 18:18 NIV

While we may find comfort in being Christians, being a Christian has not made us perfect. There are still many strongholds within us. Rare is the Christian who is not limited by at least one of the following strongholds: unbelief, cold love, fear, pride, unforgiveness, lust, greed, or any combination of these, as well as the possibility of many others. Bondage is the result of giving the devil a measure of control and living under that control. We must humble ourselves and seek help. For until one is willing to admit that he needs deliverance, he will never be free from strongholds.[48]

According to Ephesians 4:26–27, it is possible to "*give the devil a foothold*" by harboring sins like anger in our hearts. The Bible warns us that the demonic spirit will constantly work in the sons of disobedience (Ephesians 2:2). Standing firm in our faith, relying on the Holy Spirit, meditating on the Word of God, and being persistent in prayer can help us to resist the evil one (1 Peter 5:8– 9; Ephesians 6:10–16).

Lies:

Father, I praise You, for You are the God of truth. Lord, Your Word says that You desire truth in our inmost being (Psalm 51:6a). Lord, please forgive (CHILD'S NAME) for all his/her lies. Your Word says that Satan is the father of lies (John 8:44b). If (CHILD'S NAME) has yielded to Satan's lies in any area of life, I bind it in Jesus's name. Help (CHILD'S NAME) to discern the voice of the Lord. I break off the spirit of deception, which is rooted in lies. I release the Spirit of truth to invade his/her life and set him/her free. Please enable (CHILD'S NAME) to walk in the truth. In Jesus's name, Amen!

Doubt:

Lord, please forgive (CHILD'S NAME) for the moments he/she doubted Your Word. Your Word says if we do not stand firm in your faith, we will not stand at all (Isaiah 7:9b). I bind the spirit of doubt in (CHILD'S NAME) and release the Spirit of faith that comes through reading the Word of God (Romans 10:17). Lord, by Your grace, make (CHILD'S NAME) to be firm in faith. Your Word says that everything is possible for one who believes (Mark 9:23b). Please help

(CHILD'S NAME) overcome his/her unbelief. In Jesus's name, Amen!

Pride:

Lord, Your Word says that to fear the Lord is to hate evil and that You hate pride and arrogance (Proverbs 8:13). Please help (CHILD'S NAME) to have a healthy fear and remove pride and arrogance in his/her life. If pride has hardened (CHILD'S NAME)'s heart in any way (Daniel 5:20), please forgive him/her. I bind the spirit of pride in him/her and allow the Holy Spirit to invade (CHILD'S NAME)'s heart to walk humbly before God. Lord, Your Word says You oppose the proud but give grace to the humble (James 4:6). Please break those areas where pride is rooted in (CHILD'S NAME)'s life and give grace to stay humble (1 Peter 5:5b). In Jesus's name, Amen!

Lust:

Lord, Your Word says that the lust of the flesh, the lust of the eyes, and the pride of life come not from the Father but from the world (1 John 2:16). (CHILD'S NAME)'s body is a temple of the Holy Spirit. (CHILD'S NAME) is not his/her own. (CHILD'S NAME) was bought at a price. (CHILD'S NAME) is redeemed by the blood of Jesus (Ephesians 1:7). Lord, give (CHILD'S NAME) a desire to honor You with his/her body (1 Corinthians 6:19–20). I bind the spirit of lust in (CHILD'S NAME) and allow the love of God to invade his/her life. Lord, please enable CHILD'S NAME) to put to death whatever belongs to the earthly nature (Colossians 3:5). In Jesus's name, Amen!

Depression:

Lord, I surrender (CHILD'S NAME) into Your hands. He/She often battles with feelings of depression. If any medical issue causes this depression, please help (CHILD'S NAME) stabilize while he/she takes medicine. If this depression is because of any spirit that disrupts his/her normal life, I pray against it. Let the enemy be defeated in Jesus's name. Your Word encourages us that the joy of the Lord is our strength (Nehemiah 8:10b). Help (CHILD'S NAME) to rejoice in Your presence. As You heal (CHILD'S NAME), let his/her experience become a testimony and hope for many who battle with depression. In Jesus's name, Amen!

Addiction:

Lord, You know that (CHILD'S NAME) is battling with this addiction. As a child of God, (CHILD'S NAME) is not under law, but under grace. Therefore, I confess that this addiction does not have authority to rule over (CHILD'S NAME)'s life (Romans 6:14). Help (CHILD'S NAME) not to be a slave to sin, but a slave to obedience, which leads to righteous living (Romans 6:16b). Lord, please intervene in (CHILD'S NAME)'s life and set him/her free. Your Word says that You set the captives free (Isaiah 61:1b). I believe in

Your Word and proclaim that (CHILD'S NAME) is free by the name of Jesus, power of the Holy Spirit, power in Your Word, and through the blood of Jesus. Give (CHILD'S NAME) Your grace to take every thought captive to make it obedient to Christ (2 Corinthians 10:5). In Jesus's name, Amen!

Fear:

Lord, Your Word says that You did not give us a spirit of fear, but of power, love, and self-control (2 Timothy 1:7). Lord, as You know (CHILD'S NAME) struggles with fear of people, fear of the unknown, fear of death, fear of failure, fear of rejection, fear of loneliness, and more. Impart in (CHILD'S NAME) Your love that casts out fear (1 John 4:18). Pour out Your Holy Spirit upon (CHILD'S NAME) that brings freedom from fear (2 Corinthians 3:17). I believe in Your Word that nothing is impossible with You (Luke 1:37). I thank You that You can deliver (CHILD'S NAME) from the spirit of fear. In Jesus's name, Amen!

Suicide:

Lord, You want Your children to live a happy and fulfilled life with purpose. (CHILD'S NAME) struggles with the thoughts of suicide very often. Your Word says that the enemy comes only to kill, steal, and destroy, but You want us to enjoy life and have it in abundance (John 10:10). In You, (CHILD'S NAME) lives and has his/her being (Acts

17:28a). (CHILD'S NAME) may have feelings of not being heard or not having his/her feelings validated. Lord, please change the hopeless situation that (CHILD'S NAME) is in and give him/her a glimpse of the bright future that You have in store for him/her. Please fill (CHILD'S NAME) with all joy and peace as he/she believes so that he/she may overflow with hope by the power of the Holy Spirit (Romans 15:13). In Jesus's name, Amen!

Self-harm:

Lord, You came to give life to the full. Thank You for Your death so that we may enjoy life. I surrender (CHILD'S NAME) into Your hands, and You know him/her inside out. Many times, he/she cuts himself/herself and bleeds leaving scars on his/her skin. Lord, You know the reason behind his/her damaging action. If (CHILD'S NAME) is continuing this habit because he/she thinks that he/she deserves it, please replace those thoughts with an awareness of the punishment You took in Your body on the cross so that we would be set free (1 Peter 2:24). Or if this kind of self-harm is due to any emotional conflict, help (CHILD'S NAME) to understand that You are aware of all his/her ways (Psalm 139) and that he/she is accepted and valuable in Your eyes. Deliver him/her by the power of Your Holy Spirit and give him/her a godly fear that protects him/her from self-harm. In Jesus's name, Amen!

Rejection:

Lord, You promised us that You would never leave us nor forsake us. As (CHILD'S NAME) struggles with rejection very often, declare Your truth over him/her that he/she belongs to You and that he/she is loved by You. Father, Your Word says that Jesus was rejected by men but was chosen and precious before God (1 Peter 2:4). When (CHIILD'S NAME) battles with the sense of rejection, remind him/her that he/she is the son/daughter of the Most High. Open his/her eyes to understand that he/she is precious in Your sight. Reveal to (CHILD'S NAME) the plans and purpose You have for him/her, to prosper and give him/her hope and a future (Jeremiah 29:11). In Jesus's name, Amen!

Anxiety:

Lord, I surrender (CHILD'S NAME) into Your hands. As Your Word says in 1 Peter 5:7, help (CHILD'S NAME) to cast all his/her anxieties on You because You care for him/her. I bind the spirit of anxiety that constantly attacks (CHILD'S NAME)'s mind. Father, give (CHILD'S NAME) the peace that surpasses all understanding (Philippians 4:7). Lord, please grant (CHILD'S NAME) the grace he/she needs to rely on Your Word and trust in You to experience the perfect peace in his/her life. Release the Spirit of worship in his/her life. Lord, You are the God who gives beauty for ashes and the Spirit of joy for sorrow (Isaiah 61:3a). Turn his/her sorrow into joy (John 16:20b). In Jesus's name, Amen!

Fear of Death:

Lord, Your Word says that all things were created by You and that nothing is hidden from Your eyes (Hebrews 4:13). Lord, You know and understand that (CHILD'S NAME) is struggling with the fear of death. Father, please help (CHILD'S NAME) to believe that he/she is created for Your glory (Isaiah 43:7a). Whenever (CHILD'S NAME) is afraid of death, please remind him/her of Your Word that says I will not die but live and declare the works of the Lord (Psalm 118:17) Master, by Your grace, enable (CHILD'S NAME) to live under Your Lordship and build a strong prayer life and overcome the traps of the enemy. In Jesus's name, Amen!

Decree:

I declare and decree that (CHILD'S NAME) is more than a conqueror through Jesus Christ Who loves him/her (Romans 8:37).

Additional Scripture References to Get Free from Addictions:

- "'*Not by might nor by power, but by My Spirit,' Says the Lord of hosts*" (Zechariah 4:6b).
- "*Therefore if the Son makes you free, you shall be free indeed*" (John 8:36).
- "*The yoke will be destroyed because of the anointing oil*" (Isaiah 10:27b).

- *"You will know the truth, and the truth will set you free"* (John 8:32 NLT).
- *"They conquered him by the blood of the Lamb and by the word of their testimony"* (Revelation 12:11a HCSB).

Part VII

For Their Impact

DAY 28

Prayer to Influence Others

Make good use of every opportunity you have, because these are evil days.

—Ephesians 5:16 GNT

You don't have to be in a high-profile occupation to be a person of influence. In fact, if your life in any way connects with other people, you are an influencer. Everything you do at home, at church, at school, or in your job has an impact on the lives of other people. Without influence, there is no success. Even if you've had a negative effect on others in the past, you can turn that around and make your impact a positive one."[49]

Apostle Paul says, *"Don't copy the behavior and customs of this world"* (Romans 12:2a NLT). We must use every opportunity we have to influence others. "All of God's people are ordinary people who have been made extraordinary by the purpose He has given them."[50]

> "If you are not actively pursuing the person you want to be, then you are pursuing the person you don't want to be."
>
> —Theodore Roosevelt

Prayer:

Heavenly Father, I thank You for all the gifts and talents you have placed in (CHILD'S NAME). Please pour out Your favor upon (CHILD'S NAME) and strengthen his/her relationship with You. Lord, enable (CHILD'S NAME) to model a lifestyle of integrity for others. Help (CHILD'S NAME) to be the salt and light in this world (Matthew 5:13–14). Empower (CHILD'S NAME) to have a heart of love in serving those around him/her (Galatians 5:13b). Please fill (CHILD'S NAME)'s heart with Your love to lead others to Christ. Lord, help him/her not to conform to the patterns of this world (Romans 12:2), but rather to reflect the character of Christ in everything he/she does. Lord, teach (CHILD'S NAME) to set an example in speech, in conduct, in love, in faith, and in purity (1 Timothy 4:12). Give him/her grace to be sensitive to the needs of others. Remove from (CHILD'S NAME) the feelings of inadequacy and give him/her the boldness to influence others.

Decree:

I declare and decree that (CHILD'S NAME) will use every opportunity to influence others for Christ and set an example to others (Ephesians 5:16).

Additional Scripture References to Influence Others:

- *"Do not neglect to do good and to share what you have, for such sacrifices are pleasing to God"* (Hebrews 13:16 ESV).
- *"Let your light so shine before men, that they may see your good works and glorify your Father in heaven"* (Matthew 5:16).
- *"Do not be overcome by evil but overcome evil with good"* (Romans 12:21 NIV).
- *"One who is righteous is a guide to his neighbor, but the way of the wicked leads them astray"* (Proverbs 12:26 ESV).

DAY 29

Prayer for a Life of Integrity

Even children are known by the way they act, whether their conduct is pure, and whether it is right.

—Proverbs 20:11 NLT

Today, we live in a world that says, in many ways, "if you make a good impression, that's really all that matters." But you will never be a man or woman of God if that's your philosophy. Never. You cannot fake it with the Almighty God. He is not impressed with externals. He always focuses on the inward qualities, those things that take time and discipline to cultivate.[51]

Integrity does not mean to be perfect. It does not mean we don't make any mistakes. Integrity means authenticity and being real. When you have integrity, you do the right thing, and you do it for the right reason. You have unmixed, pure motives. You're sincere and straightforward in every area of your life and with all people.[52]

Prayer:

Lord, thank you for Your faithful love toward (CHILD'S NAME). Lord, Your Word says that You test the heart and delight in integrity (1 Chronicles 29:17a). Father, by Your power make (CHILD'S NAME) a person of integrity. Let his/her life align with Your Word. Please forgive (CHILD'S NAME) if he/she has compromised his/her values in his/her actions and words. To help (CHILD'S NAME) live with integrity, teach him/her to follow the example of Christ (John 13:15). Lord, grant him/her a pure and undivided heart. Father, give (CHILD'S NAME) a heart of integrity that portrays the life of Joseph. Empower him/her to pursue what is good. Father, according to Your Word, establish his/her steps to walk with integrity, do what is right, and speak the truth (Psalm 15). Strengthen (CHILD'S NAME) to stand by his/her principles no matter what the consequences. Equip (CHILD'S NAME) to advance Your kingdom; use him/her for Your glory. In Jesus's name, Amen!

Decree:

I declare and decree that (CHILD'S NAME) will walk with integrity and follow the instructions of the Lord (Psalm 119:1).

Additional Scripture References for Integrity:

- *"Whoever walks in integrity walks securely, but he who makes his ways crooked will be found out"* (Proverbs 10:9 ESV).
- *"The righteous man walks in his integrity; His children are blessed after him"* (Proverbs 20:7).

- *"Vindicate me, O Lord, For I have walked in my integrity. I have also trusted in the Lord; I shall not slip"* (Psalm 26:1).
- *"Until I die, I will not give up my integrity"* (Job 27:5b NASB).
- *"And you yourself must be an example to them by doing good works of every kind. Let everything you do reflect the integrity and seriousness of your teaching"* (Titus 2:7 NLT).

Part VIII

Marriage

DAY 30

Prayer for a Life Partner

And this is the confidence that we have toward him, that if we ask anything according to his will, he hears us.

—1 John 5:14 ESV

Marriage is the one covenant that is binding until death. So, it's necessary to begin interceding for our children's marriage. It seems obvious that our children want to marry a Christian man or woman. However, if they allow their hearts to become entangled with emotional ties towards an unbelieving person-it could be very difficult for them to walk away. Never underestimate the power of a praying parent that can reach far into future generations.[53]

As we pray for their future mates, we can be specific in our prayers. James 4:2b says, "*You do not have, because you do not ask God.*" It is not wrong to be specific with God, particularly when our requests line up with God's will for our children's lives. God loves to answer our prayers (Matthew 7:11). One of our prayers could be that our kids will marry people who love God with all their heart, soul, mind, and strength (Mark 12:30).

Prayer:

Lord God, You said, *"It is not good for the man to be alone. I will make a helper suitable for him"* (Genesis 2:18 NIV). We pray for Your divine favor and godly connection in (CHILD'S NAME)'s life. Lord, we desire that Your Word will become the final authority in (CHILD'S NAME)'s future. Our merciful Father, please do not allow (CHILD'S NAME) to be yoked together with an unbeliever (2 Corinthians 6:14). If (CHILD'S NAME)'s relationship will lead him/her to the wrong path, please instruct him/her to submit to Your perfect will. Cause (CHILD'S NAME) to be willing to wait for Your perfect timing. Please develop a heart in (CHILD'S NAME) that is sensitive to Your voice in choosing the right partner. Lord, we trust that You will make everything beautiful in its time (Ecclesiastes 3:11a). We allow You to guide him/her to the right person at the right time. Help (CHILD'S NAME) to not settle for anything less than what You have in store for him/her.

Prayer for Married Life:

Lord, we pray for the young adults who have started their lives together in marriage. Your word says that a cord of three strands is not quickly broken (Ecclesiastes 4:12). We invite Your presence into their marriage. Please strengthen the bond between them and align their hearts with Your will. We pray that they will consider and look out for each other's interests. Give them the humility to be submissive to each other in the fear of God (Ephesians 5:21). Father, by Your grace, help them not to hold onto anger or hold grudges against each other (Ephesians 4:26). Lord, enable them to forgive one another and keep the unity of the Spirit through the bond of peace (Ephesians 4:3). Lord, enhance the understanding of commitment in their marriage and draw them closer to You. Father, give them wisdom to understand and acknowledge their differences. Please help them to be sensitive to each other's needs. Let their marriage become rooted and grounded in God's love (Ephesians 3:17) and built on a firm foundation. In Jesus's name, Amen!

Decree:

We declare and decree that God has a plan to prosper (CHILD'S NAME) and give him/her a future and hope (Jeremiah 29:11).

Additional Scripture References for Marriage:

- *"And over all these virtues put on love, which binds them all together in perfect unity"* (Colossians 3:14 NIV).
- *"An excellent wife who can find? She is far more precious than jewels"* (Proverbs 31:10 ESV).

- *"Therefore a man shall leave his father and mother and hold fast to his wife, and the two shall become one flesh"* (Ephesians 5:31 ESV).
- *"Do not be unequally yoked together with unbelievers. For what fellowship has righteousness with lawlessness? And what communion has light with darkness"* (2 Corinthians 6:14)?
- *"What therefore God has joined together, let not man separate"* (Mark 10:9 ESV).

Part IX

Blessings

DAY 31

Aaronic Blessings

The Lord bless you and keep you; the Lord make His face shine upon you and be gracious to you; the Lord lift up His countenance upon you and give you peace.

—Numbers 6:24–26

As Aaron spoke these words of blessing, he did so according to God's command. It is clear that the Lord is the source of this blessing. God's Words are His actions. God does things by speaking. In the beginning 'God said' and "it was" (Genesis 1). When it is God Who speaks, His Word defines reality. God's spoken Word assures His people that it will be so.[54]

We have a High Priest in Heaven, Jesus Christ, who is of an even higher order than Aaron. God designated Jesus to be a High Priest (Hebrews 5:4, 10). In His name, by faith, we can also decree and declare the Priestly Blessing to our children. For *"He has made us a Kingdom of priests for God his Father"* (Revelation 1:6a NLT).

Parental blessing has the power to bring God's blessings upon our children. Our blessings will have a lasting impact on them because words have creative power. *"Death and life are in the power of the tongue"* (Proverbs 18:21a).

Prayer

We thank You Father for all the blessings in Your Word. We bless (CHILD'S NAME) in Your Name and ask that You would bless him/her and keep him/her. We pray that You would give him/her good health. Bless (CHILD'S NAME) when he/she comes in and when he/she goes out (Deuteronomy 28:6). We thank You that You deliver (CHILD'S NAME) from all attacks of the enemy and protect him/her from all danger. We pray that no weapon the enemy tries to use against (CHILD'S NAME) can prosper (Isaiah 54:17a). Lord, cover (CHILD'S NAME) with favor as with a shield (Psalm 5:12). We pray that (CHILD'S NAME) will increase in wisdom and find favor and good success in the sight of God and man (Proverbs 3:4). Give (CHILD'S NAME) a sound mind and enable him/her to think about things that are true and noble (Philippians 4:8). Lord, give (CHILD'S NAME) Your strength and bless him/her with peace (Psalm 29:11). We pray that (CHILD'S NAME) may prosper in all things and be in good health. In Jesus's name, Amen!

Decree:

We declare and decree that (CHILD'S NAME) will be the head, not the tail and that he/she will be above, not below (Deuteronomy 28:13).

Additional Scripture References for Blessings:

- *"Look, I am with you, and I will watch over you wherever you go"* (Genesis 28:15a BSB).
- *"You will be blessed in the city and blessed in the country"* (Deuteronomy 28:3 NIV).
- *"May God be gracious to us and bless us, and make his face to shine upon us"* (Psalm 67:1 ESV).
- *"I will be gracious to whom I will be gracious and will show mercy on whom I will show mercy"* (Exodus 33:19b ASV).

Appendix

Additional Resources for Parents

Bounds, E. M. *The Necessity of Prayer*. Merchant Books, 2015.

Chapman, Gary, and Ross Campbell. *The 5 Love Languages of Children*. Moody Publishers, 2012.

Fuller, Cheri. *The One Year Praying through the Bible*. Tyndale Momentum, 2003.

Townsend, John. *Boundaries with Teens: When to Say Yes, How to Say No*. Zondervan, 2006.

Scripture Index

Introduction

"For we do not have a High Priest who cannot sympathize with our weaknesses, but was in all points tempted as we are, yet without sin" (Hebrews 4:15).

"Now this is the confidence that we have in Him, that if we ask anything according to His will, He hears us" (1 John 5:14).

"Likewise the Spirit also helps in our weaknesses. For we do not know what we should pray for as we ought, but the Spirit Himself makes intercession for us with groanings which cannot be uttered. Now He who searches the hearts knows what the mind of the Spirit is, because He makes intercession for the saints according to the will of God" (Romans 8:26–27).

"By faith we understand that the worlds were framed by the word of God, so that the things which are seen were not made of things which are visible" (Hebrews 11:3).

DAY 1: Prayer for a Heart to Seek God

"And this is eternal life, that they may know You, the only true God, and Jesus Christ whom You have sent" (John 17:3).

"And as long as he sought the Lord, God gave him success" (2 Chronicles 26:5b NIV).

"For whoever comes [near] *to God must* [necessarily] *believe that God exists and that He rewards those who* [earnestly and diligently] *seek Him"* (Hebrews 11:6b AMP).

"For You, Lord, have not forsaken those who seek You" (Psalm 9:10b).

"Blessed are those who keep His testimonies, who seek Him with the whole heart" (Psalm 119:2b)!

"Now may the Lord direct your hearts into the love of God and into the patience of Christ" (2 Thessalonians 3:5).

"I will put My fear in their hearts so that they will not depart from Me" (Jeremiah 32:40b).

"And you will seek Me and find Me, when you search for Me with all your heart" (Jeremiah 29:13).

DAY 2: Prayer for Humility

"But when his heart was lifted up, and his spirit was hardened in pride, he was deposed from his kingly throne, and they took his glory from him" (Daniel 5:20).

"Be kind and compassionate to one another, forgiving each other, just as in Christ God forgave you" (Ephesians 4:32 NIV).

"But made Himself of no reputation, taking the form of a bondservant, and coming in the likeness of men" (Philippians 2:7).

"Let nothing be done through selfish ambition or conceit, but in lowliness of mind let each esteem others better than himself" (Philippians 2:3).

"But He gives more grace. Therefore He says: "God resists the proud, but gives grace to the humble" (James 4:6).

"Be still, and know that I am God; I will be exalted among the nations, I will be exalted in the earth" (Psalms 46:10)!

DAY 3: Prayer to Forgive Others

"Not proud, rude or selfish, not easily angered, and it keeps no record of wrongs" (1 Corinthians 13:5 CJB).

"Now hope does not disappoint, because the love of God has been poured out in our hearts by the Holy Spirit who was given to us" (Romans 5:5).

"For if you forgive men their trespasses, your heavenly Father will also forgive you" (Matthew 6:14).

"And be kind to one another, tenderhearted, forgiving one another, even as God in Christ forgave you" (Ephesians 4:32).

DAY 4: Prayer for Obedience

"Honor your father and your mother, that your days may be long upon the land which the Lord your God is giving you" (Exodus 20:12).

"And being found in appearance as a man, He humbled Himself and became obedient to the point of death, even the death of the cross" (Philippians 2:8).

"I have no greater joy than to hear that my children walk in truth" (3 John 1:4).

"My sheep hear My voice, and I know them, and they follow Me" (John 10:27).

"If you are willing and obedient, You shall eat the good of the land" (Isaiah 1:19).

"Now it shall come to pass, if you diligently obey the voice of the Lord your God, to observe carefully all His commandments which I command you today, that the Lord your God will set you high above all nations of the earth" (Deuteronomy 28:1).

DAY 5: Prayer for Gratitude

"In all your ways acknowledge Him, and He shall direct your paths" (Proverbs 3:6).

"In everything give thanks; for this is the will of God in Christ Jesus for you" (1 Thessalonians 5:18).

"Every good gift and every perfect gift is from above, and comes down from the Father of lights, with whom there is no variation or shadow of turning" (James 1:17).

"Do all things without murmurings and disputings" (Philippians 2:14 KJV).

"Whoever offers praise glorifies Me" (Psalm 50:23a).

DAY 6: Prayer for a Sound Mind

"For those who live according to the flesh set their minds on the things of the flesh, but those who live according to the Spirit, the things of the Spirit" (Romans 8:5).

"Finally, brethren, whatever things are true, whatever things are noble, whatever things are just, whatever things are pure, whatever things are lovely, whatever things are of good report, if there is any virtue and if there is anything praiseworthy—meditate on these things" (Philippians 4:8).

"And do not be conformed to this world, but be transformed by the renewing of your mind" (Romans 12:2a).

"And the peace of God, which surpasses all understanding, will guard your hearts and minds through Christ Jesus" (Philippians 4:7).

"Casting down arguments and every high thing that exalts itself against the knowledge of God, bringing every thought into captivity to the obedience of Christ" (2 Corinthians 10:5).

DAY 7: Prayer for Healing from Insecurity

"I will praise You, for I am fearfully and wonderfully made; Marvelous are Your works, and that my soul knows very well" (Psalm 139:14).

"Therefore, if anyone is in Christ, he is a new creation; old things have passed away; behold, all things have become new" (2 Corinthians 5:17).

"Just as He chose us in Him before the foundation of the world, that we should be holy and without blame before Him in love" (Ephesians 1:4).

"You shall also be a crown of glory in the hand of the Lord, and a royal diadem in the hand of your God" (Isaiah 62:3).

"He will rejoice over you with gladness, He will quiet you with His love, He will rejoice over you with singing" (Zephaniah 3:17b).

DAY 8: Prayer to Find Their Identity in Christ

"For I know the thoughts that I think toward you, says the Lord, thoughts of peace and not of evil, to give you a future and a hope" (Jeremiah 29:11).

"Don't be conformed to the patterns of this world, but be transformed by the renewing of your minds so that you can figure out what God's will is—what is good and pleasing and mature" (Romans 12:2 CEB).

"And the world is passing away, and the lust of it; but he who does the will of God abides forever" (1 John 2:17).

"Therefore, if anyone is in Christ, he is a new creation; old things have passed away; behold, all things have become new" (2 Corinthians 5:17).

"Yet in all these things we are more than conquerors through Him who loved us" (Romans 8:37).

"For we are His workmanship, created in Christ Jesus for good works, which God prepared beforehand that we should walk in them" (Ephesians 2:10).

DAY 9: Prayer to Overcome Fear

"I sought the Lord, and He heard me, and delivered me from all my fears" (Psalm 34:4).

"Fear not, for I am with you" (Isaiah 43:5a).

"There is no fear in love; but perfect love casts out fear, because fear involves torment. But he who fears has not been made perfect in love" (1 John 4:18).

"Peace I leave with you, My peace I give to you; not as the world gives do I give to you. Let not your heart be troubled, neither let it be afraid" (John 14:27).

"Whenever I am afraid, I will trust in You" (Psalm 56:3).

"Have I not commanded you? Be strong and of good courage; do not be afraid, nor be dismayed, for the Lord your God is with you wherever you go" (Joshua 1:9).

DAY 10: Prayer for Protection from the Enemy

"He who dwells in the secret place of the Most High shall abide under the shadow of the Almighty" (Psalm 91:1).

"For this purpose the Son of God was manifested, that He might destroy the works of the devil" (1 John 3:8b).

"Have I not commanded you? Be strong and of good courage; do not be afraid, nor be dismayed, for the Lord your God is with you wherever you go" (Joshua 1:9).

"The Lord shall preserve you from all evil; He shall preserve your soul" (Psalm 121:7).

"And they overcame him by the blood of the Lamb and by the word of their testimony, and they did not love their lives to the death" (Revelation 12:11).

DAY 11: Prayer to Reach Their God-given Potential

"No one can receive anything unless God gives it from heaven" (John 3:27b NLT).

"Therefore, my brothers and sisters, make every effort to confirm your calling and election. For if you do these things, you will never stumble" (2 Peter 1:10 NIV).

"Do you see a man who excels in his work? He will stand before kings; He will not stand before unknown men" (Proverbs 22:29).

"As each one has received a special gift, employ it in serving one another as good stewards of the multifaceted grace of God" (1 Peter 4:10 NASB).

"I can do all things through Christ who strengthens me" (Philippians 4:13).

DAY 12: Prayer for Wisdom

"So that you incline your ear to wisdom, and apply your heart to understanding" (Proverbs 2:2).

"The fear of the Lord is the beginning of wisdom, and the knowledge of the Holy One is understanding" (Proverbs 9:10).

"If any of you lacks wisdom, let him ask of God, who gives to all liberally and without reproach, and it will be given to him" (James 1:5).

"I will give you such words and wisdom that none of your enemies will be able to refute or contradict what you say" (Luke 21:15 GNT).

"Then this Daniel was preferred above the presidents and princes, because an excellent spirit was in him; and the king thought to set him over the whole realm" (Daniel 6:3 KJV).

"The fear of the Lord is the beginning of wisdom" (Proverbs 9:10a).

DAY 13: Prayer for Godly Friendship

"But I have called you friends, for all things that I heard from My Father I have made known to you" (John 15:15b).

"He who walks with wise men will be wise, but the companion of fools will be destroyed" (Proverbs 13:20a).

"Do not judge, so that you will not be judged" (Matthew 7:1 NASB).

"He who covers his sins will not prosper, but whoever confesses and forsakes them will have mercy" (Proverbs 28:13).

"Noah was a just man, perfect in his generations. Noah walked with God" (Genesis 6:9b).

DAY 14: Prayer for God's Favor

"With favor You will surround him as with a shield" (Psalm 5:12b).

"I entreated Your favor with my whole heart; be merciful to me according to Your word" (Psalm 119:58).

"The Lord bestows grace and favor and honor; No good thing will He withhold from those who walk uprightly" (Psalm 84:11b AMP).

"And Jesus increased in wisdom and stature, and in favor with God and men" (Luke 2:52).

DAY 15: Prayer to Protect Children from Indoctrination in School

"Train up a child in the way he should go, and when he is old he will not depart from it" (Proverbs 22:6).

"You shall diligently keep the commandments of the Lord your God, His testimonies, and His statutes which He has commanded you" (Deuteronomy 6:17).

"But the Lord is faithful, who will establish you and guard you from the evil one" (2 Thessalonians 3:3).

"Behold, I give you the authority to trample on serpents and scorpions, and over all the power of the enemy, and nothing shall by any means hurt you" (Luke 10:19).

"My sheep hear My voice, and I know them, and they follow Me" (John 10:27).

DAY 16: Prayer for Salvation

"To open their eyes, in order to turn them from darkness to light, and from the power of Satan to God, that they may receive forgiveness of sins" (Acts 26:18a).

"That if you confess with your mouth the Lord Jesus and believe in your heart that God has raised Him from the dead, you will be saved" (Romans 10:9).

"For "whoever calls on the name of the Lord shall be saved" (Romans 10:13).

"And I will give you a new heart, and I will put a new spirit in you. I will take out your stony, stubborn heart and give you a tender, responsive heart" (Ezekiel 36:26 NLT).

"For by grace you have been saved through faith, and that not of yourselves; it is the gift of God" (Ephesians 2:8).

"I will give them an undivided heart and put a new spirit in them; I will remove from them their heart of stone and give them a heart of flesh" (Ezekiel 11:19 NIV).

"In humility correcting those who are in opposition, if God perhaps will grant them repentance, so that they may know the truth" (2 Timothy 2:25).

"Salvation is found in no one else, for there is no other name under heaven given to mankind by which we must be saved" (Acts 4:12 NIV).

"All your children shall be taught by the Lord, and great shall be the peace of your children" (Isaiah 54:13).

DAY 17: Prayer for Fear of the Lord

"The fear of the Lord is to hate evil" (Proverbs 8:13a).

"He will fulfill the desire of those who fear Him; He also will hear their cry and save them" (Psalm 145:19).

"The fear of the Lord leads to life, and he who has it will abide in satisfaction; He will not be visited with evil" (Proverbs 19:23).

"The fear of the Lord is the beginning of wisdom" (Proverbs 9:10a).

"By humility and the fear of the Lord are riches and honor and life" (Proverbs 22:4).

DAY 18: Prayer to Love God's Word

"By faith we understand that the worlds were framed by the word of God, so that the things which are seen were not made of things which are visible" (Hebrews 11:3).

"For you have been born again, not of perishable seed, but of imperishable, through the living and enduring word of God" (1 Peter 1:23 NIV).

"He sent His word and healed them and delivered them from their destruction" (Psalm 107:20).

"Your words were found, and I ate them, and Your word was to me the joy and rejoicing of my heart" (Jeremiah 15:16a).

"For the word of God is living and powerful, and sharper than any two-edged sword, piercing even to the division of soul and spirit, and of joints and marrow, and is a discerner of the thoughts and intents of the heart" (Hebrews 4:12).

"Heaven and earth will pass away, but My words will by no means pass away" (Matthew 24:35).

"Sanctify them by Your truth. Your word is truth" (John 17:17).

"How can a young man cleanse his way? By taking heed according to Your word" (Psalm 119:9).

"Your word I have hidden in my heart, that I might not sin against You" (Psalm 119:11).

"My soul melts from heaviness; Strengthen me according to Your word" (Psalm 119:28).

"So then faith comes by hearing, and hearing by the word of God" (Romans 10:17).

"Your word is a lamp to my feet and a light to my path" (Psalm 119:105).

"This Book of the Law shall not depart from your mouth, but you shall meditate in it day and night, that you may observe to do according to all that is written in it. For then you will make your way prosperous, and then you will have good success" (Joshua 1:8).

DAY 19: Prayer for Healthy Emotions

"But the fruit of the Spirit is love, joy, peace, patience, kindness, goodness, faithfulness, gentleness, self-control; against such things there is no law" (Galatians 5:22–23 ESV).

"Cease from anger, and forsake wrath; Do not fret—it only causes harm" (Psalm 37:8).

"A peaceful mind gives life to the body, but jealousy rots the bones" (Proverbs 14:30 CEB).

"But let patience have its perfect work, that you may be perfect and complete, lacking nothing" (James 1:4).

"For to be carnally minded is death, but to be spiritually minded is life and peace" (Romans 8:6).

"And the peace of God, which surpasses all understanding, will guard your hearts and minds through Christ Jesus" (Philippians 4:7).

DAY 20: Prayer for Faith in God

"For I say, through the grace given to me, to everyone who is among you, not to think of himself more highly than he ought to think, but to think soberly, as God has dealt to each one a measure of faith" (Romans 12:3).

"And we know that all things work together for good to those who love God, to those who are the called according to His purpose" (Romans 8:28).

"For everyone born of God overcomes the world. This is the victory that has overcome the world, even our faith" (1 John 5:4 NIV).

"Looking unto Jesus, the author and finisher of our faith" (Hebrews 12:2a).

"But without faith it is impossible to please Him, for he who comes to God must believe that He is, and that He is a rewarder of those who diligently seek Him" (Hebrews 11:6).

"So then faith comes by hearing, and hearing by the word of God" (Romans 10:17).

"For in it the righteousness of God is revealed from faith to faith; as it is written, "The just shall live by faith" (Romans 1:17).

"In whom we have boldness and confident access through faith in Him [that is, our faith gives us sufficient courage to freely and openly approach God through Christ]" (Ephesians 3:12 AMP).

"For whatever is born of God overcomes the world. And this is the victory that has overcome the world—our faith" (1 John 5:4).

"Jesus said to him, "If you can believe, all things are possible to him who believes" (Mark 9:23).

DAY 21: Prayer for Righteous Living

"If we confess our sins, He is faithful and just to forgive us our sins and to cleanse us from all unrighteousness" (1 John 1:9).

"Hear my prayer, O Lord, give ear to my supplications! In Your faithfulness answer me, and in Your righteousness" (Psalm 143:1).

"Therefore, if anyone is in Christ, he is a new creation; old things have passed away; behold, all things have become new" (2 Corinthians 5:17).

"But no, all have turned away; all have become corrupt. No one does good, not a single one" (Psalm 53:3 NLT)!

"But now we are seeing the righteousness of God declared quite apart from the Law [though amply testified to by both Law and Prophets]*—it is a righteousness imparted to, and operating in, all who have faith in Jesus Christ"* (Romans 3:21 J. B. Philips New Testament).

"God presented Christ as a sacrifice of atonement, through the shedding of his blood—to be received by faith. He did this to demonstrate his righteousness" (Romans 3:25a NIV).

"Where is boasting then? It is excluded. By what law? Of works? No, but by the law of faith. Therefore we conclude that a man is justified by faith apart from the deeds of the law" (Romans 3:27–28).

"For He made Him who knew no sin to be sin for us, that we might become the righteousness of God in Him" (2 Corinthians 5:21).

"For if by the one man's offense death reigned through the one, much more those who receive abundance of grace and of the gift of righteousness will reign in life through the One, Jesus Christ" (Romans 5:17).

DAY 22: Prayer for the Work of the Holy Spirit

"In the last days I will send My Spirit on all men. Then your sons and daughters will speak God's Word" (Joel 2:28a NLV).

"However, when He, the Spirit of truth, has come, He will guide you into all truth" (John 16:13a).

"Now hope does not disappoint, because the love of God has been poured out in our hearts by the Holy Spirit who was given to us" (Romans 5:5).

"God also testified to it by signs, wonders and various miracles, and by gifts of the Holy Spirit distributed according to his will" (Hebrews 2:4 NIV).

"And I will pray the Father, and He will give you another Helper, that He may abide with you forever" (John 14:16).

"But they rebelled and grieved His Holy Spirit" (Isaiah 63:10a).

"Now the Lord is the Spirit, and where the Spirit of the Lord is, there is freedom" (2 Corinthians 3:17 NIV).

"Likewise the Spirit also helps in our weaknesses. For we do not know what we should pray for as we ought, but the Spirit Himself makes intercession for us with groanings which cannot be uttered. Now He who searches the hearts knows what the mind of the Spirit is, because He makes intercession for the saints according to the will of God" (Romans 8:26–27).

"The prayer of a righteous person is powerful and effective" (James 5:16b NIV).

DAY 23: Prayer for Their Walk with God

"He has shown you, O man, what is good; And what does the Lord require of you but to do justly, to love mercy, and to walk humbly with your God" (Micah 6:8)?

"And Enoch walked with God" (Genesis 5:24a).

"Can two walk together, unless they are agreed" (Amos 3:3)?

"Your ears shall hear a word behind you, saying, 'This is the way, walk in it,' whenever you turn to the right hand or whenever you turn to the left" (Isaiah 30:21).

"But if we walk in the light as He is in the light, we have fellowship with one another, and the blood of Jesus Christ His Son cleanses us from all sin" (1 John 1:7).

DAY 24: Prayer for Deliverance from Manipulative and Controlling Spirit

"When he speaks a lie, he speaks from his own resources, for he is a liar and the father of it" (John 8:44b).

"It is not in man who walks to direct his own steps" (Jeremiah 10:23b).

"Again I say to you that if two of you agree on earth concerning anything that they ask, it will be done for them by My Father in heaven" (Matthew 18:19).

"Set examples for each other in showing respect" (Romans 12:10b CJB).

DAY 25: Freedom from Addiction to Social Media

"Ah, Lord God! Behold, You have made the heavens and the earth by Your great power and outstretched arm. There is nothing too hard for You" (Jeremiah 32:17).

"If we say that we have no sin, we deceive ourselves, and the truth is not in us" (1 John 1:8).

"Have You not made a hedge around him, around his household, and around all that he has on every side" (Job 1:10a)?

"A person without self-control is like a city with broken-down walls" (Proverbs 25:28 NLT).

"O Lord our God, other lords besides you have ruled over us" (Isaiah 26:13a ESV).

"The yoke shall be destroyed because of the anointing" (Isaiah 10:27b KJV).

DAY 26: Prayer to Break Every Chain from Demonic Influences

"That serpent of old, called the Devil and Satan, who deceives the whole world" (Revelation 12:9b).

"We know that we are children of God and that the world around us is under the control of the evil one" (1 John 5:19 NLT).

"No one knows the things of God except the Spirit of God" (1 Corinthians 2:11b).

"But he who is spiritual judges all things" (1Corinthians 2:15a).

"He personally carried our sins in his body on the cross so that we can be dead to sin and live for what is right. By his wounds you are healed" (1 Peter 2:24 NLT).

"In the same way, you must think of yourselves as dead to the power of sin. But Christ Jesus has given life to you, and you live for God" (Romans 6:11 CEV).

"For the law of the Spirit of life in Christ Jesus has made me free from the law of sin and death" (Romans 8:2).

"Now the Lord is the Spirit, and where the Spirit of the Lord is, there is freedom" (2 Corinthians 3:17 ESV).

"The spirit who now works in the sons of disobedience" (Ephesians 2:2b).

"I command you, come out of him and enter him no more" (Mark 9:25b)!

"He sent His word and healed them" (Psalm 107:20a).

"For freedom Christ has set us free; stand firm therefore, and do not submit again to a yoke of slavery" (Galatians 5:1 ESV).

"You are of God, little children, and have overcome them, because He who is in you is greater than he who is in the world" (1 John 4:4).

"Yet in all these things we are more than conquerors through Him who loved us" (Romans 8:37).

DAY 27: Freedom from Addiction and All Kinds of Spirits

"Be angry, and do not sin": do not let the sun go down on your wrath, nor give place to the devil" (Ephesians 4:26–27).

"You were following the course and fashion of this world [were under the sway of the tendency of this present age], *following the prince of the power of the air.* [You were obedient to and under the control of] *the* [demon] *spirit that still constantly works in the sons of disobedience* [the careless, the rebellious, and the unbelieving, who go against the purposes of God]" (Ephesians 2:2b AMPC).

"Be sober, be vigilant; because your adversary the devil walks about like a roaring lion, seeking whom he may devour. Resist him, steadfast in the faith" (1 Peter 5:8–9a).

Lies:

"Behold, You desire truth in the innermost being" (Psalm 51:6a AMP).

"When he speaks a lie, he speaks from his own resources, for he is a liar and the father of it" (John 8:44b).

Doubt:

"If you do not stand firm in your faith, then you will not stand at all" (Isaiah 7:9b HCSB).

"So then faith comes by hearing, and hearing by the word of God" (Romans 10:17).

"Everything is possible for one who believes" (Mark 9:23b NIV).

Pride:

"The fear of the Lord is to hate evil; Pride and arrogance and the evil way and the perverse mouth I hate" (Proverbs 8:13).

"But when his heart was lifted up, and his spirit was hardened in pride, he was deposed from his kingly throne, and they took his glory from him" (Daniel 5:20).

"But he gives more grace. Therefore it says, "God opposes the proud but gives grace to the humble" (James 4:6 ESV).

"God resists the proud, but gives grace to the humble" (1 Peter 5:5b).

Lust:

"For all that is in the world—the lust of the flesh, the lust of the eyes, and the pride of life—is not of the Father but is of the world" (1 John 2:16).

"In Him we have redemption through His blood, the forgiveness of sins, according to the riches of His grace" (Ephesians 1:7).

"Or do you not know that your body is the temple of the Holy Spirit who is in you, whom you have from God, and you are not your own? For you were bought at a price; therefore glorify God in your body and in your spirit, which are God's" (1 Corinthians 6:19–20).

"Put to death, therefore, whatever belongs to your earthly nature: sexual immorality, impurity, lust, evil desires and greed, which is idolatry" (Colossians 3:5 NIV).

Depression:

"The joy of the Lord is your strength" (Nehemiah 8:10b).

Addiction:

"For sin shall not have dominion over you, for you are not under law but under grace" (Romans 6:14).

"He has sent me to bind up the brokenhearted, to proclaim freedom for the captives and release from darkness for the prisoners" (Isaiah 61:1b NIV).

"Casting down arguments and every high thing that exalts itself against the knowledge of God, bringing every thought into captivity to the obedience of Christ" (2 Corinthians 10:5).

Fear:

"For God has not given us a spirit of fear, but of power and of love and of a sound mind" (2 Timothy 1:7).

"There is no fear in love; but perfect love casts out fear, because fear involves torment. But he who fears has not been made perfect in love" (1 John 4:18).

"For the Lord is the Spirit, and wherever the Spirit of the Lord is, there is freedom" (2 Corinthians 3:17 NLT).

"For with God nothing will be impossible" (Luke 1:37).

Suicide:

"The thief comes only in order to steal and kill and destroy. I came that they may have and enjoy life, and have it in abundance [to the full, till it overflows]" (John 10:10 AMPC).

"For in Him we live and move and have our being" (Acts 17:28a).

"Now may the God of hope fill you with all joy and peace in believing, that you may abound in hope by the power of the Holy Spirit" (Romans 15:13).

Self-harm:

"Who Himself bore our sins in His own body on the tree, that we, having died to sins, might live for righteousness—by whose stripes you were healed" (1 Peter 2:24).

Rejection:

"Coming to Him as to a living stone, rejected indeed by men, but chosen by God and precious" (1 Peter 2:4).

"For I know the thoughts that I think toward you, says the Lord, thoughts of peace and not of evil, to give you a future and a hope" (Jeremiah 29:11).

Anxiety:

"Cast all your anxiety on him because he cares for you" (1 Peter 5:7 NIV).

"And the peace of God, which surpasses all understanding, will guard your hearts and minds through Christ Jesus" (Philippians 4:7).

"To those who have sorrow in Zion I will give them a crown of beauty instead of ashes. I will give them the oil of joy instead of sorrow, and a spirit of praise instead of a spirit of no hope" (Isaiah 61:3a NLV).

"Your sorrow will be turned into joy" (John 16:20b).

Fear of Death:

"And there is no creature hidden from His sight, but all things are naked and open to the eyes of Him to whom we must give account" (Hebrews 4:13).

"Everyone who is called by My name, whom I have created for My glory" (Isaiah 43:7a).

"I shall not die, but live, and declare the works of the Lord" (Psalm 118:17).

"Yet in all these things we are more than conquerors through Him who loved us" (Romans 8:37).

DAY 28: Prayer to Influence Others

"You are the salt of the earth; but if the salt loses its flavor, how shall it be seasoned? It is then good for nothing but to be thrown out and trampled underfoot by men. You are the light of the world. A city that is set on a hill cannot be hidden" (Matthew 5:13–14).

"Through love serve one another" (Galatians 5:13b).

"And do not be conformed to this world, but be transformed by the renewing of your mind, that you may prove what is that good and acceptable and perfect will of God" (Romans 12:2).

"Let no one despise your youth, but be an example to the believers in word, in conduct, in love, in spirit, in faith, in purity" (1 Timothy 4:12).

"Making the best use of the time, because the days are evil" (Ephesians 5:16 ESV).

DAY 29: Prayer for a Life of Integrity

"I know also, my God, that You test the heart and delight in uprightness and integrity" (1 Chronicles 29:17a AMP).

"For I have given you an example, that you should do as I have done to you" (John 13:15).

"Joyful are people of integrity, who follow the instructions of the Lord" (Psalm 119:1 NLT).

DAY 30: Prayer for a Life Partner and Marriage

"If you then, being evil, know how to give good gifts to your children, how much more will your Father who is in heaven give good things to those who ask Him" (Matthew 7:11)!

"And you must love the Lord your God with all your heart, all your soul, all your mind, and all your strength" (Mark 12:30 NLT).

"The Lord God said, "It is not good for the man to be alone. I will make a helper suitable for him" (Genesis 2:18 NIV).

"Do not be unequally yoked together with unbelievers. For what fellowship has righteousness with lawlessness? And what communion has light with darkness" (2 Corinthians 6:14)?

"He has made everything beautiful in its time" (Ecclesiastes 3:11a).

"Though one may be overpowered by another, two can withstand him. And a threefold cord is not quickly broken" (Ecclesiastes 4:12).

"Submitting to one another in the fear of God" (Ephesians 5:21).

"If indeed you have heard Him and have been taught by Him, as the truth is in Jesus" (Ephesians 4:21).

"Be angry, and do not sin": do not let the sun go down on your wrath" (Ephesians 4:26).

"Being diligent to keep the unity of the Spirit in the bond of peace" (Ephesians 4:3 NASB).

"That Christ may dwell in your hearts through faith; that you, being rooted and grounded in love" (Ephesians 3:17).

"For I know the thoughts that I think toward you, says the Lord, thoughts of peace and not of evil, to give you a future and a hope" (Jeremiah 29:11).

DAY 31: Aaronic Blessings

"And no one takes this honor on himself, but he receives it when called by God, just as Aaron was" (Hebrews 5:4 NIV).

"Was designated by God to be high priest in the order of Melchizedek" (Hebrews 5:10 NIV).

"Blessed shall you be when you come in, and blessed shall you be when you go out" (Deuteronomy 28:6).

"No weapon formed against you shall prosper" (Isaiah 54:17a).

"For You, O Lord, will bless the righteous; With favor You will surround him as with a shield" (Psalm 5:12).

"So you will find favor and good success in the sight of God and man" (Proverbs 3:4 ESV).

"Finally, brothers and sisters, whatever is true, whatever is noble, whatever is right, whatever is pure, whatever is lovely, whatever is admirable—if anything is excellent or praiseworthy—think about such things" (Philippians 4:8 NIV).

"The Lord will give strength to His people; The Lord will bless His people with peace" (Psalm 29:11).

"The Lord will make you the head and not the tail. If you listen to the Laws of the Lord your God which I tell you today and be careful to obey them, you will only be above and not below" (Deuteronomy 28:13 NLV).

Topical Index

Acknowledgments

I am grateful to the staff at Lucid Books Publishing company who worked with me throughout the book buildout process. Their involvement, wise counsel, and helpful perspective made our vision a reality. I pray that they will continue to stand out as a beacon of light to influence the world through their mission.

I thank Valter DeSouza for his contributions to improving the manuscript.

I am grateful for Kelly Prendiville whose editing enhanced the book's clarity.

I sincerely appreciate Barbara Winbush's final editing, which significantly enriched the content of this book.

We would love to hear from you! Please share with us how this prayer book has blessed you by emailing your comments and suggestions to praytorestore@outlook.com

Endnotes

1 E. M. Bounds, The Complete Works of E. M. Bounds on Prayer (Baker Books, 1990), 153.

2 Jim Cymbala, Life-Changing Prayer, DVD (HarperChristian Resources, 2018).

3 Charles Stanley, "Life Principle 8: Fight Your Battles on Your Knees," In Touch Ministries, November 1, 2019, https://www.intouch.org/watch/sermons/life-principle-8-fight-your-battles-on-your-knees.

4 Stanley, "Seeking the Lord: Our Hunger for God is Both Satisfied and Deepened as We Spend Time in His Word." In Touch Ministries, 2022, www.intouch.org/read/daily-devotions/seeking-the-lord.

5 John Piper, "Do not Love the World," Desiring God Ministries, 1985, www.desiringgod.org/messages/do-not-love-the-world.

6 Kurt Selles, "Walking with Humility," Reframe Ministries, 2023, todaydevotional.com/devotions/walking-with-humility.

7 David C. Cooper, "Timeless Truths in Changing Times" (Discover Life Ministries, 2004), 315.

8 Vaneetha Rendall Risner, "We Cannot Cling to Bitterness and God," Desiring God Ministries, 2021, www.desiringgod.org/articles/we-cannot-cling-to-bitterness-and-god.

9 Thea Leunk, "The Power of Forgiveness," Reframe Ministries, 2013, todaydevotional.com/devotions/the-power-of-forgiveness-2013-06-20.

10 Chuck Lynch, "The Ripple Effects of Bitterness," The Balm of Gilead Ministries (blog), February 16, 2017, https://balmofgilead.co/category/ripple-effects-of-bitterness/.

11 John Piper, "The Pleasure of God in Obedience (Sanctification & Growth)," Desiring God Ministries, 1987, www.desiringgod.org/messages/the-pleasure-of-god-in-obedience.

12 Oswald Chambers, Obedience or Independence, The Wisdom Center, 2023, thewisdomcentre-bnj.org/obedience-or-independence-by-oswald-chambers/.

13 Derek Prince, "Stopping to Say "Thanks": Let us Show Gratitude," Derek Prince Ministries, 2024, www.global.derekprince.com/devotions/c-11-11.

14 Joyce Meyer, "The Power of a Renewed Mind: We Can Choose Our Thoughts and Think Things on Purpose," Joyce Meyers Ministries, accessed November 2023, joycemeyer.org/grow-your-faith/articles/the-power-of-a-renewed-mind.

15 Jentezen Franklin, "You Have a Sound Mind!(1)," Jentezen Franklin Ministries, May 11, 2015, jentezenfranklin.org/daily-devotions/you-have-a-sound-mind-1.

16 Donna Gibbs, Silencing Insecurity: Believing God's Truth about You (Revell, 2018), 10–11, 13, 17–18.

17 Rick Warren, "Be Confident in Whose You Are," June 6, 2018, pastorrick.com/devotional/english/full-post/be-confident-in-whose-you-are/.

18 Chap Clark, and Tim Clinton, The Quick-Reference Guide to Counseling Teenagers (Baker Books, 2010), 172.

19 Alex McFarland, "The Source of Self-Worth," Focus on the Family, 2010, www.focusonthefamily.ca/content/the-source-of-self-worth,

20 Warren, "Choose Faith over Fear," November 27, 2021, pastorrick.com/choose-faith-over-fear-4/.

21 Billy Graham, "God's Divine Love Is—Fearless," Billy Graham Evangelistic Association, 2014, billygraham.org/story/divine-love-is-fearless/.

22 Franklin, "Spiritual Warfare (2)," Jentezen Franklin Ministries, 2013, jentezenfranklin.org/daily-devotions/spiritual-warfare-2/.

23 Cooper, Timeless Truths, 257.

24 Robert McGee, The Search for Significance (Thomas Nelson, 2003), 74.

25 Cooper, Timeless Truths, 158.

26 Michael A. Milton, "What is Wisdom? (and How to Get It)," Bible Study Tools, 2019, www.biblestudytools.com/bible-study/topical-studies/what-is-wisdom-and-how-to-get-it.html.

27 Alistair Begg, "True Friendship," Truth for Life, 2024, www.truthforlife.org/devotionals/alistair-begg/1/13/2024/.

28 Stanley, "How Do We Find Favor With God?" In Touch Ministries, 2020, www.intouch.org/read/daily-devotions/how-do-we-find-favor-with-god.

29 Ruth Grandlund, Encouraging Parents to Stand Firm Against Unbiblical Ideologies in the Public Square, Association of Certified Biblical Scholars, August 23, 2023, biblicalcounseling.com/resource-library/articles/the-parents-biblical-fight-against-the-public-indoctrination-of-children/.

30 Michael Youssef, "Ask Dr. Youssef: How Can I Protect My Children from Indoctrination within the Public School System?" Leading the Way, March 3, 2022, www.ltw.org/read/articles/2022/03/ask-dr-youssef-how-can-i-protect-my-children-from-indoctrination-within-the-public-school-system.

31 Dutch Sheets, How to Pray for Lost Loved Ones (Bethany House Publishers, 2001), 56, 63.

32 A. W. Tozer, The Knowledge of the Holy (General Press, 1961), 72.

33 Nancy Missler, Private Worship: The Key to Joy (The King's Highway Ministries, 2002), 78–79.

34 Chambers, "The 12 Most Challenging Oswald Chambers Quotes, Relevant Magazine.com, November 13, 2015, https://relevantmagazine.com/faith/12-most-challenging-oswald-chambers-quotes/.

35 Bounds, Complete Works on Prayer, 66–67, 71.

36 Piper. "Life Hangs on the Word of God," September 25 Devotional, Desiring God Ministries, www.desiringgod.org/articles/life-hangs-on-the-word-of-god.

37 Tozer, "Satan's Greatest Weapon—AW Tozer," Deeper Christian Quotes, June 29, 2023, https://deeperchristianquotes.com/satans-greatest-weapon-aw-tozer/.

38 Michael S. Houdman, "What Happens after Death?" Got Questions Ministries, 2017, www.gotquestions.org/what-happens-after-death.html.

39 Wesley L. Duewel, Measure Your Life: 17 Ways to Evaluate Your Life from God's Perspective (Authentic Books, 1992), 83, 85.

40 Stanley, "Our Righteousness: We Could Never Earn Our Way into God's Presence, But We Can Receive His Gift of Salvation," In Touch Ministries, 2020, www.intouch.org/read/daily-devotions/our-righteousness.

41 Bounds, Complete Works on Prayer, 282–284.

42 Graham, "What Does It Mean To Walk With God?" Billy Graham Evangelistic Association, 2017, billygraham.org/answer/what-does-it-mean-to-walk-with-god/.

43 Tony Evans, "The Walk of Faith." Tony Evans, 2023, tonyevans.org/enoch-the-walk-of-faith/.

44 Timothy L. Sanford, "How to Deal Wisely with Manipula tive People," Focus on the Family, June 29, 2020, www.focusonthefamily.com/get-help/how-to-deal-with-manipulative-people/.

45 Andy Crouch, The Tech-Wise Family: Everyday Steps for Putting Technology in Its Proper Place (Baker Books, 2017), 140–141.

46 Dannah Gresh, "Teens Using Media: Why Social Media Shouldn't Define Your Teen," Focus on the Family, 2017, accessed April 2024, www.focusonthefamily.com/parenting/why-social-media-shouldnt-define-your-teen/#h-identity-in-christ.

47 Jack Ashcraft, "Are Tarot Cards Evil? What Should Christians Know?" Christianity.com, updated March 26, 2024, www.christianity.com/wiki/cults-and-other-religions/what-should-christians-know-about-tarot-cards.html.

48 Francis Frangipane, The Three Battlegrounds (Arrow Publi cations, 2006), 36–37.

49 John C. Maxwell and Jim Dornan, Becoming a Person of Influence (Thomas Nelson, Inc, 1997), 3, 9.

50 Chambers, My Utmost for His Highest (Discovery House Publishers, 1992), October 25th Devotional.

51 Chuck Swindoll, "A Man of Integrity," Insight for Living, December 13, 2019, www.insight.org/resources/daily-devotional/individual/a-man-of-integrity1.

52 Warren, "Do You Act the Same in Public and in Private?" May 18, 2023, pastorrick.com/do-you-act-the-same-in-public-and-in-private/.

53 Crystal McDowell, "Praying for Your Children's Future Spouses," What Christians Want to Know, accessed November 2023, www.whatchristianswanttoknow.com/praying-for-your-childrens-future-spouses/.

54 Michael J. Glodo, The Lord Bless You and Keep You (Crossway, 2023), 35–36.

About the Author

Leonie Shankar was born and raised in South India. About 25 years ago, she moved to the US and now lives in New Hampshire with her wonderful husband and their son. Her passion for helping women through life's struggles led her to pursue a Master's Degree in Human Services Counseling for Marriage and Family at Liberty University. Leonie's life experiences have taught her to rely on God's power and promises in parenting. She firmly believes that every parent can claim God's promises and exercise God-given authority in raising their children.

Additional Prayer Points

Additional Prayer Points

www.ingramcontent.com/pod-product-compliance
Lightning Source LLC
Chambersburg PA
CBHW072003040426
42447CB00009B/1464

* 9 7 8 1 6 3 2 9 6 7 3 8 1 *